T0329204

THE DIOSCURI

IN THE

CHRISTIAN LEGENDS

THE DIOSCURI

IN THE

CHRISTIAN LEGENDS

BY

J. RENDEL HARRIS, M.A.

FELLOW OF CLARE COLLEGE, CAMBRIDGE

London

C. J. CLAY AND SONS,

CAMBRIDGE UNIVERSITY PRESS WAREHOUSE,

AVE MARIA LANE.

1903

CAMBRIDGE
UNIVERSITY PRESS

University Printing House, Cambridge CB2 8BS, United Kingdom

Cambridge University Press is part of the University of Cambridge.

It furthers the University's mission by disseminating knowledge in the pursuit of education, learning and research at the highest international levels of excellence.

www.cambridge.org
Information on this title: www.cambridge.org/9781107497764

First published 1903
First paperback edition 2015

A catalogue record for this publication is available from the British Library

ISBN 978-1-107-49776-4 Paperback

CHAPTER I.

FLORUS AND LAURUS.

In a recent examination of certain Byzantine calendars of Saints, chiefly of a S. Italian type, I was struck by the frequency of the occurrence of the names of SS. Florus and Laurus: and it was natural to enquire who they were and why they were so popular. The first step in the investigation was the inference from the names that *Florus and Laurus were twins.*

All over the world and apparently in every age there has been a tendency to give twin names to twin children, the slight modification in the consonants or the vowels of the two names being sufficient to distinguish one from the other, while the general similarity in the sounds indicates that they are twins: the variation in the sound is the equivalent of the red thread by which one of a certain pair of twins is differentiated from the other in the Hebrew legend. As instances of these names in their simplest form we might take Yama and Yami from the Rig-veda, Romulus and Remus from the Roman History, or Baltram and Sintram from Germanic mythology. And even where the records or legends do not positively affirm that the persons are twins, we can infer the fact from the names without any direct statement. Thus it is extremely difficult not to believe that Huz and Buz (Gen. xxii. 21) are twins (a hypothesis which is not contradicted by the statement 'Huz his firstborn, and Buz his brother'); the same thing is true of the first two names in the triad, Huppim, Muppim and Ard (Gen. xlvi. 21).

A more striking case is that of Tryphaena and Tryphosa (Rom. xvi. 12) in the New Testament, for here either form is a feminine to the masculine Τρυφων, according as the accent falls on the first or second syllable.

Even where the equivalence of the names is not apparent to the eye nor sensible to the ear, it is often quite clear to the reflecting mind.

For instance, the famous twins of the Serapeum at Memphis were known by the names of Taues and Taous, and there ought to have been no difficulty in recognizing them as twin-sisters, even if they were not persistently called αἱ δίδυμαι. But then the same things may be said of the young ladies who were ibis-wardens at Thebes[1], although one of them was called Tathautis and the other Taeibis; for we can dissect out of their names when the feminine prefix is removed (a) the god Thoth, (b) the sacred ibis which is his outward and visible equivalent.

A similar case in the Greek mythology is that of the two brethren Lynceus and Idas who kill Castor and Pollux, or rather who kill Castor, for Pollux is one of the immortals. It has been suspected by scholars that the conflict in question relates to a struggle for supremacy between two independent local cults of the Great Twin-brethren; and certainly when we examine the names of the supposed Dioscuri of Messene, Lynceus and Idas, we find the idea of sharp-sightedness, not only in the well-known Lynceus but also in his brother; and this encourages the belief that they are twins, though the names at first seem to be remote. Probably with a better knowledge of philology, we should be able to make the still desiderated nexus between the names of Castor and Pollux.

So, without any reference to the Acta Sanctorum, we were able to infer that Florus and Laurus were twins.

The next step in the investigation occurred when I was reading Tolstoi's *Peace and War*[2], and stumbled on the following conversation between two Russian peasants:

---

[1] Document known as the 'Money Bill from Thebes' in the facsimiles of the Paleographical Society.

[2] Eng. Trans. IV. 49.

'Certainly I say my prayers,' replied Pierre. 'But what was that about Frola and Laura?'

'Why,' swiftly replied Platon, 'that's the horses' saints. For we must have pity on the cattle.'

Here we see that in Russian folk-lore, *Florus and Laurus are the patron saints of horses.*

Putting this statement by the side of the previous suggestion that they were twins, we have at once the hypothesis that *Florus and Laurus are 'the great twin-brethren, to whom the Dorians pray.'*

And now it is time to turn to the hagiologists, and see whether we can confirm these statements. The day on which Florus and Laurus are honoured is August 18th. On this day the Συναξαριστής[1] begins its discourse with the words, 'These saints were twin-brethren, stonemasons by trade, who had learnt their craft from S. Patroclus and S. Maximus, who also themselves suffered martyrdom for Christ' (οὗτοι οἱ ἅγιοι ἦσαν μὲν ἀδελφοὶ δίδυμοι, λιθοξόοι δὲ τὴν τέχνην, ἐκμαθόντες αὐτὴν παρὰ τοῦ ἁγίου Πατρόκλου καὶ ἁγίου Μαξίμου, μαρτυρησάντων καὶ αὐτῶν διὰ τὸν Χριστόν).

This verifies for us our first hypothesis, viz. that Florus and Laurus were twins; but seems to repel the second suggestion that we had to do with patron-saints of horses, for how should stonemasons be in the brotherhood or confraternity of horsemen? They, at all events, even if master-builders, would go on foot. Moreover, the day is not what we should at first expect; for there have been reasons for believing that the festival of the battle of the Lake Regillus at Rome, when the Dioscuri are honoured, viz. the 15th of July, is an older festival than the battle itself, the case being perhaps parallel to those occurrences in the Acta Sanctorum where deliverances which occur on a saint's day are credited to the saint[2].

[1] I quote from the popular Greek edition published at Zante in 1868.

[2] Albert in his *Étude sur le culte de Castor et Pollux* proceeds on the assumption that the battle of the Lake Regillus is the starting point for the Roman worship of the Twins: to which we can by no means agree. He is wrong also in his development of the cult from two human heroes. We shall see the matter very differently.

However, let us look around us, before plunging deeper into
the Acts of the Martyrdom.

We shall find from the Roman Martyrology that August 18th
is the day on which the Roman Church honours Helena the
mother of Constantine: setting side by side the two statements
that on August 18th

    (a)   the Greek Church honours Florus and Laurus,

    (b)   the Roman Church honours Helena,

we are encouraged to believe that the Helena referred to is a
displacement of the sister of the Dioscuri, and that the two
separate cults are part of a single original worship.

For the worship of Helen along with the Dioscuri in the
great centre of their cult, Sparta, we need only quote Euripides,
Helena 1666,

> Ὅταν δὲ κάμψῃς καὶ τελευτήσῃς βίον,
> θεὸς κεκλήσει, καὶ Διοσκούρων μέτα
> σπονδῶν μεθέξεις.

The same thing is proved for outlying centres, as in the
case of Agrigentum, for which we have the testimony of Pindar,
Ol. iii. 1,

> Τυνδαρίδαις τε φιλοξείνοις ἁδεῖν
> καλλιπλοκάμῳ θ᾽ Ἑλένᾳ
> κλεινὰν Ἀκράγαντα γεραίρων εὔχομαι—

and is confirmed by numismatic testimony from a number of
unexpected quarters.

But perhaps the most striking case of divided honours
between the Twins and their sister, is the common esteem in
which they were held all over the Mediterranean by sailors.
Thus Euripides says in his *Orestes* 1636, of Helen,

> Κάστορί τε Πολυδεύκει τ᾽ ἐν αἰθέρος πτυχαῖς
> σύνθακος ἔσται, ναυτίλοις σωτήριος.

This common honour was divided under the two heads of
fear and trust, and Helen's share was, for the most part, and in
spite of Euripides, the former. The electric discharges which
are sometimes seen on the masts and yards of ships were
named after the twins and their sister. According to Pliny

the single discharge was named after Helena, and was *dira ac minax*, while a divided flame was named after Castor and Pollux and was held to be propitious. In the middle ages the Helena-fire is known as the fire of St Elmo, and it is reasonably certain that St Elmo is only a corruption of the name of Helen, though some have tried to connect it with a S. Erasmus[1].

Now that we have established the antiquity of the Helena-cult by the side of that of the Dioscuri, we are not at all surprised that the same day (Aug. 18th) should have been marked for the festivals of Florus and Laurus, and of Helen the mother of Constantine. And we are reasonably secure in our conclusion as to the identity of Florus and Laurus with the Twins, in view of the appearance of Helena on the same day.

We shall, then, assume that the argument, so far, is clear, and we shall be able to turn to the Acta Sanctorum and see what actually happened.

The general drift of the martyrdom is as follows: Florus and Laurus were twin-brothers, stonecutters, who had learnt their craft from the martyrs Patroclus and Maximus. Leaving Byzantium, they migrated to the province of Dardania where they settled in a city named Ulpiana, and endeavoured to get work as quarrymen from the governor of the province, whose name was Lycion or Lycon. He sends them to Licinius the son of queen Elpidia; and Licinius engages them to build a temple, of which he draws them a plan and for which he furnishes them with funds. The saints take the money and spend it on the poor; by day they work at the building, by night they give themselves to prayer. When the work is nearly finished, in which they have angelic help, the chief priest of the temple, whose name is Merentius, becomes a believer in Christ, his son Athanasius having been cured of blindness by the twin-brethren. Thereupon the idols of the temple are dishonoured and destroyed. The temple is consecrated as a Christian church, with many pious hymns and the kindling of many lights.

---

[1] For the dangers which attend the Helena fire, we may compare Solinus 18. 1 *Helenae sidus navigantibus perniciosissimum*: and of course, Horace

Fratres Helenae, lucida sidera.

When Licinius hears of this, he first of all burns alive all the poor people who had received the charities of the saints, and had helped to break up the statues of the gods. Then he bound Florus and Laurus to a wheel and either flayed or beat them (ἐδάρησαν). Then he sends them back to Lycion, who pitches them into a dry well where they perish. Some time after their bones are recovered and honoured, and work miracles for the faithful. Such is, in brief, the story of the blessed twin-brethren, Florus and Laurus.

Now when we read a legend of this kind, we have to separate from it whatever can be directly credited to the invention of the hagiologist, and we have then to try and determine how much history is left, what real characters are involved, how far the places and the people can be identified, and what elements in the martyrdom can be believed. In our case the problem is simplified by our knowledge that the cult of Florus and Laurus replaces some form or other of the cult of the Dioscuri. The recognition of this fact at once affects our judgment as to the historical character of the incidents related.

For instance, the change of the cult being conceded, it follows at once that there has been a change in the religious building where the cult was practised. The legends tell us so quite plainly; a pagan temple was converted into a Christian church through the conversion of the chief priest of the temple and his son. The story says that the saints were set to build a temple and that they actually built a church. We may accept as history the statement that in a certain town in Illyricum a temple, perhaps of the Dioscuri themselves, was turned into a Christian church under the patronage of SS. Florus and Laurus. Thus far, there is no need to regard these as real persons: they may be real, but on the other hand they may be only the Dioscuri over again. Along with the Dioscuri their sister Helen was honoured, for S. Helena's day is the same as that of Florus and Laurus. S. Helena is real and historical; whether Florus and Laurus are so, is an open question.

The first thing we are told of the twins is that they were stonemasons. We have to ask whether this is historical, or whether the hagiologist made them stonemasons in order that they might build the temple which he had in mind. Or, to put another suggestion which comes from the identification of the twins with the Dioscuri, perhaps Castor and Pollux may have been stonemasons and temple-builders.

If the last supposition can be verified the whole story becomes legend, and all history has evaporated except the single fact of the conversion of a heathen temple into a Christian church. We proceed to enquire whether there is any foundation for the suggestion that there was a nexus between the Dioscuri and the work of stonecutting or the guild of the stonecutters.

At the first glance the supposition seems a very unlikely one. We should have expected a breath of the salt sea or a reek of the stable from the neighbourhood of the Dioscuri, but there is no mention of the sea or of sailors, and no allusion to horse-care or horse-craft. On the other hand the Russian folk-lore shows that this pair of Dioscuri could be known by other characteristics than naval ones, and, indeed, when we reflect that the ritual displaced was evidently that of an inland town, the reason for maritime features has disappeared. Moreover, since the legend does not credit the saints with the power to drive or tame horses, but only with the art of stonecutting, we are obliged to enquire whether this may not have been one of the many benevolent arts exercised by Castor and Polydeuces. Is there, then, any evidence for associating the great twin-brethren with the craft which is said to have been practised by the little twin-brethren? Do they work in stone and build temples? The answer to this question is in the affirmative. We have the authority of Pausanias for the statement that in the southern part of the Peloponnesus there was a temple which had been built by the Dioscuri. The passage is as follows:

On the right of Gythium is Las, distant two furlongs from the sea and forty from Gythium. The town is now built between the mountains of Ilium, Asia and Coracadium, but it used to stand on the top of Mount Asia....Amongst the ruins is a temple of Athena surnamed Asia; they say that it was made by Pollux and Castor when they came back from Colchis,

and that there is a sanctuary of Athena Asia in Colchis also. I know that
the sons of Tyndareus went on the voyage with Jason; but that the
Colchians worship Athena Asia is a statement that I give on the authority
of the people of Las, from whom I had it.

(Pausanias III. 24. 5.)

Here, then, is the first corroboration of the suggestion that
in popular belief the Dioscuri were credited with the art of the
stonemason and the temple-builder. And we may reasonably
infer that the knowledge of their skill in building was not
confined to Arcadia or Messene, but that in other places they
were honoured for their architectural skill, and perhaps credited
with actual proofs of it, in the shape of temples which they
were supposed to have constructed[1]. With this inference the
historical element in the legend of Florus and Laurus evapo-
rates away, except so far as relates to the change of religion in
a certain town in Illyricum. For if the twin-brethren are the
Dioscuri, and their craft is also the craft of the Dioscuri, we
have nothing left in the legend that can be called their own.
Patroclus and Maximus are fictitious, for they too are stonemasons. The story becomes either reminiscences of the adventures of the Dioscuri, or it is mere hagiologic invention of
the conventional type.

And now let us look a little closer into the information
which Pausanias gives us as to the opinions and beliefs of the
people of Las. Their faith that the Dioscuri had been amongst
them and had built a temple near by was associated with
another belief that the Dioscuri had sacked their city on their
return from the Argonautic expedition.

This latter belief is an etymological creation, by which it
was sought to explain a curious title by which the great twin-
brethren were known, viz. the title of Lapersai: this was
interpreted to mean 'ravagers of Las.' Accordingly we find
in Strabo the following statement:

---

[1] Something similar, as we shall see presently, occurs in the case of the
Theban twins, Amphion and Zethus, who first sack the city and then rebuild it.
At least Amphion plays the part of builder, while Zethus makes music; in
other forms of the legend both brothers are masons. Should we compare
Romulus and Remus?

τὴν δὲ Λᾶν οἱ Διόσκουροί ποτε ἐκ πολιορκίας ἐλεῖν ἱστοροῦνται, ἀφ' οὗ
δὴ Λαπέρσαι προσηγορεύθησαν, καὶ Σοφοκλῆς λέγει που·
νὴ τὼ Λαπέρσα, νὴ τὸν Εὐρώταν τρίτον,
νὴ τοὺς ἐν ˮΑργει καὶ κατὰ Σπάρτην θεούς.
(Strabo VIII. 364.)

The same explanation of the name Lapersai is found in Stephanus
of Byzantium, sub voce Λά.

Λὰ πόλις Λακωνική· Λυκόφρων· καὶ Λᾶν περήσεις. Ταύτην ἑλόντες οἱ
Διόσκουροι Λαπέρσαι ἐκλήθησαν......κεῖται δὲ ἐπὶ πέτρας ὑψηλῆς· διὸ Λὰ
καλεῖται· οἱ κατοικοῦντες Λαοί.
Λαπέρσα θηλυκῶς· ὄρος Λακωνικῆς, οὗ μέμνηται Ῥιανὸς ἐν Ἡλιακῶν πρώτῳ.
ἀπὸ τῶν Λαπερσῶν Διοσκούρων.

Here we find the geographer giving the conventional explanation; but he adds another suggestion that the word Λᾶς
or Λά means rock, which is probably correct; and also gives us
the further information of another mountain which bears the
name Lapersa and which he absurdly supposed to have been
named after the Dioscuri who had themselves been named
after the former mountain. Obviously this is nothing but
word-spinning. And when we find from Tzetzes on Lycophron
that there was an Attic deme named Λαπέρσιος, we are obliged
to abandon the early explanations, and ask for some solution
which lies a little nearer to nature and a little further from the
realm of the mythologist.

Our suggestion will be that the name Λαπέρσαι is the
equivalent of stonecutters, λιθοξόοι or λατόμοι. We have
already shown from the legends of Florus and Laurus the
probability that the Dioscuri were credited with the power to
hew stone and to build temples. Is it, however, possible to
deduce this meaning from the title Lapersai? If it were,
everything would clear up as regards names of places and
people: the mountain in Laconia would be named after a
quarry in its side, the deme in Attica would be the stonecutters' ward, or at all events the ward of the Heavenly
Twins, and the Dioscuri would be known by the beneficent
art which they had taught the human race.

We observe, however, from the quotation given from
Sophocles, that the first a in Λαπέρσα is short; and it is,

therefore, impossible to identify the first syllable with Λâ. We must not search for the stonecutter in that direction.

Suppose, however, that we divide the word in another way, and make it Λαπ+ερσαι. We can at once recognize in the first syllable the root which lies behind the Latin *lapis* and the Greek λέπας. So we have only to explain the second part of the name. Here we have the analogy of the Phrygian name Lityerses, where we are advised to recognize the spirit of vegetation, under one of its many vagrant forms. The story of Lityerses, the son of a Phrygian king, and of his reaping matches against strangers whom he enticed into the harvest field and then wrapped in sheaves and beheaded, has been shown by Mannhardt and others to be the mythological form of an ancient cult of the Corn-spirit, to which parallels can be found all over the world. And it has been suggested, as we shall see presently, that the name Lityerses may mean 'the worker of the tilth,' the first half of the word being a word for 'corn,' and the latter the equivalent of the Greek -ϝεργης (as in ἐνεργής, ἀεργής). The main difficulty here is the introduction of the digamma, which at first sight seems fatal to the quantity of the *a* in Λαπέρσαι. But at least we may infer that a common termination -ερσης is in the name of the Dioscuri and in the name of the Phrygian threshing prince. That seems to be, at all events, a reasonable hypothesis.

At this point the argument passes out of my hands, and I am obliged to consult my friends in the region of philology, and ask them whether the presence of the digamma in the Greek ϝεργον implies a sound of such strength that it would be preserved after *p* in the Phrygian language or in the closely related Thracian speech. Their verdict is of the nature of a press-censor's *nihil obstat*. Dr J. H. Moulton thinks the hypothesis of an equation between Λαπέρσης and 'stone-cutter' very attractive, draws the parallel with Lityerses, but thinks the proof must be extra-philological.

Prof. Conway has examined the suggestion carefully, and writes:

After spending some time with the Phrygian and Thracian fragments I think it reasonably probable that λαπερσης is good Thracian for stone-worker.

λαπ- will be Lat. *lap-(id-)* and -ερσης will stand for -Ϝεργης (cf. ἐνεργής, ἀεργής). All I can be sure of is

(1) that original Indo-European *g* became *z* or *s* in Thracian : e.g. the fairly common suffix *zenus-, -sanus* (Αυλοζανος, Diuzenus) which is certainly parallel to Gr. -γενης, Lat. *-genus*, all meaning 'son of.'

(2) that orig. Ϝ (*ṳ*) i.e. consonant *u* remained and did not become any more solid sound (not, e.g., a labio-dental *v*)....If Λιτυ-έρσης is connected with λει-Ϝā 'corn,' it might conceivably mean 'worker of the tilth': for the *-tu-* cf. *Saturnus, Mā-tū-ta, fortuna*. But

(3) I have not found any example which proves that -πϜ- would become simply -π- in Thracian, but on general grounds it is quite likely, since precisely that same change happened in Greek (νήπιος beside νηπύτιος), Italic and Celtic....It is hard to keep a real *w* alive after a *p*. The moving power for the etymology must come from your side, but I think these points are enough to show that there are no phonetic mountains to be moved.

Thus far Dr Moulton and Prof. Conway. It will be observed that in my treatment of the fact that Florus and Laurus were stonemasons, and the inference that they are the Dioscuri in disguise, I have practically assumed, in stating the case for the resulting philological speculation, that the cult of the Dioscuri in Greece is a northern cult which has moved southward. Those who hold that Zeus himself has moved in that direction will have no difficulty in that supposition, they will say that Διος+κουροι implies that the Twins follow the migration of their Sire. But we can easily establish that the cult of the Twins belongs to the northern races from other considerations, as will be seen presently. Meanwhile let it be stated that whether the explanation of Λαπέρσα by 'twin stoneworkers' is correct or not, there is a strong suspicion, apart from all philological speculation, that we have recovered from the Florus and Laurus legend another of the many occupations of the benevolent Dioscuri. And I think we shall be able to show that in the mythological evolution of these benevolent offices the art of building stone-temples is one of the last stages of development.

It is well known that the legends of the Dioscuri are very widely diffused. For example Tacitus tells us in the *Germania* of a people in Eastern Europe (? Poland, Lithuania) who worshipped the great twin-brethren :

Apud Nahanarvalos antiquae religionis lucus ostenditur. Praesidet sacerdos muliebri ornatu : sed deos interpretatione Romana Castorem Pollucem memorant : ea vis numini, nomen Alcis. Nulla simulacra, nullum peregrinae superstitionis vestigium : ut fratres tamen, ut juvenes venerantur.

I believe the name Alcis has not yet met with an explanation. Apart from the name, Tacitus' description is sufficient to identify the worship with an early stage of the cult of the Dioscuri. And it will be observed that the worship is in a grove and not in a temple, a simple trait which recalls the earliest features of the Vedic and Indo-Germanic religion.

The statement of Tacitus is curiously confirmed by an examination of Lettish folk-songs, which constantly refer to certain 'Sons of God' who ride upon a chariot and set free the daughter of the Sun. These *dewa deli* or *Sons of God* have naturally been equated with the Διόσκουροι, and the daughter of the Sun whom they pursue and liberate is in the Greek mythology the captive Helena.

But these Lettish folk-songs furnish us with another link with the Dioscuri in a direction that had otherwise been suspected. Their language and ideas are strikingly parallel to those of the Vedic Hymns, in which we again find the great twin-brethren, under the name of Açvin (dual Açvinau). Their name shows that they have something to do with horses, and the mythology of their birth and life brings this out in all kinds of fantastic forms. It should, however, be understood that they are not horsemen in the modern sense (as we find the Dioscuri at the battle of the Lake Regillus) but horsemen in the ancient sense, when the horse was driven in a chariot. And indeed the same thing is true of the earliest forms of Greek legend; the horse-taming Castor means a horse-breaker, but not for riding, and when the pair are described as ταχέων ἐπιβήτορες ἵππων as in the Homeric Hymns, it has long been recognized that this means chariot-riders and not horse-riders in our sense of the word.

Assuming then that the Açvins of the Rig-veda are twin charioteers, we see at once that they are the Dioscuri; they appear also in the Persian religion under the name *açpinô yāvinô*, the two youths the Açpins. Their Indo-Germanic character is thus completely established[1].

In the Vedic hymns they are accompanied on their chariot by the virgin Sūryā, who is the daughter of the Sun. Here we have Helena appearing along with the twin-brethren.

What was the origin of the legend of the Dioscuri is not so important for us, as the question of the offices which they discharged to men, after they had been recognized as the θεοὶ σωτῆρες, from whom various forms of help were to be expected. It is, however, interesting to observe that the Vedic legends connect the twin-brethren with the sunrise, and that the proper time for prayer to them is just before the dawn. And the best explanation that has yet been given of their origin is that they are personifications of the morning and evening star, considered as a pair of stars, one being immortal, viz. the morning star, and the other mortal, as sinking with the sun into the dark. Hence the difference in Greek legend between Castor the mortal and Polydeuces the immortal, and hence also certain mythical inventions with regard to their birth. This identification, which is said to be due in the first instance to Bollensen[2], received an extraordinary confirmation from Mannhardt's study of the Lettish sun-myths[3], for here the Sons of God who ride upon horses are actually described as the morning and evening star. Here are one or two specimens from the Lettish songs, in a German translation:

> Warum stehen die grauen Rosse
> An der Hausthür der Sonne?
> Es sind des Gottessohnes graue Rosse
> Der freit um die Tochter der Sonne.

---

[1] Oldenberg, *Religion des Veda*, p. 43. " Nicht blos aus der vedischen Ueberlieferung, sondern auch aus derjenigen der anderen verwandten Völker, lässt sich der sichere Beweis führen, dass unsere Gottheiten ein Gemeingut aller indogermanischer Völker waren."

[2] ZDMG. 41. 496.

[3] *Zeitschrift für Ethnologie*, Vol. VII. (1875).

(Notice here how the 'Sons of God' in the plural have turned into the 'Son of God' in the singular.)

> Wessen sind die grauen Rösschen
> An Göttchens Hausthür?
> Das sind des Mondes Rösschen
> Derer die da freien um die Sonnentöchter.

Here the moon is said to own the horses: but in the following stanza it is expressly said that the moon has no horse of his own.

> So sagen die Leute,
> Der Mond habe kein eignes Rösschen;
> Der Morgenstern und der Abendstern
> Sind des Mondes Rösschen.

The frank differentiation of the morning star from the evening star, and the connexion of the pair thus imagined as horses or horsemen, should be sufficient to indicate the conclusion which Mannhardt arrives at, after an analysis of great minuteness and scientific precision[1]. As we have said above, our concern is to find out what were the friendly offices which the young heroes discharged to humanity. It may be conceded at once that we must not expect to find in the earliest mythology any traces of the building of stone temples. The Rig-veda, for example, belongs to an earlier stage than that of temple building and of temple worship.

According to Macdonnell (*Vedic Mythology* p. 49), the Açvins are celebrated in more than fifty entire hymns and in parts of several others, while their name occurs more than 400 times.

In the Rig-Veda they have come to be typically succouring divinities. They are the speediest helpers and deliverers from distress in general. They are constantly praised for such deeds. In particular, they rescue from the ocean in a ship or ships...Their rescue from all kinds of distress is a peaceful manifestation of divine grace, not a deliverance from foes in

---

[1] Mannhardt, l. c. p. 309. "Der Kundige muss bald gewahr werden, wie genau mit den lettischen Mythen von den Gottessöhnen und den Sonnentöchter oder Gottestöchter die griechischen von den beiden Dioskuren und ihre Schwester Helena übereinstimmen. Ihr Mythus ist zwar bei Homer sowohl, als auch in den Kyprien (bei Pindar), bereits durch verschiedene fremdartige Motivirungen verdunkelt, &c."

battle[1], as is generally the case with Indra....Thus they are also characteristically divine physicians, who heal diseases with their remedies, restoring sight, curing the blind, sick and maimed.

In Myriantheus (*Die Açvins*), a work which wrongly attempts to prove that the Açvins are originally the personification of the twilight, as against the identification with the morning and evening star, will be found an excellent summary from the Vedic literature of the miracles with which the Twins were credited ; as for example that

(1) they deliver from darkness:

(2) they are the authors of rejuvenescence (hence their help is sought by the aged and the emasculate):

(3) they protect in battle:

(4) they act as physicians (healing the blind, the lame &c.):

(5) they are the patrons of the bride-chamber and bestow benedictions upon the newly-married :

(6) they promote happiness in wedlock and are generally Gods of increase (under which head they are credited with the invention of the plough and with the descent of rain from heaven[2], and with the falling of the dew):

(7) they save men from storms (under this head there are numerous appeals to the Brethren as having saved from drowning a certain Bhuyyu, whom they brought to land after three days and three nights, when his friends had thrown him into the sea. He called on the Açvins and walked on the sea, without wavering. They came and took him on their chariot).

To this list of benevolences we propose to add, for a later period in the history of the cult, and not necessarily for India, the feature of their activity which came out in the foregoing analysis; viz.

(8) they teach men how to work and build in stone.

We will now apply a test to the foregoing results, by examining the Greek Menaea in order to see whether they betray any traces of acquaintance with the meaning of the legend of Florus and Laurus. If they do, we shall have a

---

[1] But cf. what is noted below under (6).

[2] E.g. "You, O Açvins, that lay enemies low, sow grain with the plough, and milk out the quickening streams of water for men."

confirmation of the correctness of our views that will be very valuable. We premise that the hymns of the Greek service in the Menaea usually incorporate the leading features in the accounts of the martyrdom, so that it will be necessary, for the test to mean anything, that the hymnologist should go beyond the accounts of the Synaxarium, by way of expansion or of explanation.

In the first place, we shall find that the saints are regarded as two luminaries in the firmament of the Church: thus:

Δύο φωστῆρες ὤφθητε νοητῷ στερεώματι τῷ τῆς ἐκκλησίας ἱερῶς ἐμπρέ-ψαντες, καὶ πᾶσαν φωτίζετε περιφανῶς τὴν κτίσιν ἀεὶ θαυματοποιίας ἀθλοφόροι βοῶντες κτέ.

Here the saints are regarded as stars, in language partly borrowed from Aeschylus *Agam.* 6,

λαμπροὺς δυνάστας ἐμπρέποντας αἰθέρι.

In the next passage that we quote, they are not only stars, but a pair equated with the evening star, or with some conspicuous pair of stars.

Ἡ θεία καὶ φωσφόρος ὄντως δυάς, Λαῦρε Φλῶρε καλλίνικοι μάρτυρες ἐν οὐρανοῖς πάντοτε Τριάδι τῇ παντουργῷ παρεστηκότες, λύτρωσιν τῶν ἁμαρ-τημάτων καὶ τῶν δεινῶν αἰτήσασθε τοῖς πίστει ὑμῶν τὴν θείαν μνήμην ἐπὶ τῆς γῆς πανηγυρίζουσι.

In a third passage the hymnologist draws on the legend of their death when thrown into the well, but immediately turns from this to say that they have been discovered and shine out again like stars in heaven.

Λάκκῳ συγκλειόμενοι καὶ ὑπὸ γῆν καλυπτόμενοι ἀπηνείᾳ δικάζοντος, θείαις εἰσηγήσεσι καὶ ἀποκαλύψει Πνεύματος Ἁγίου ἐφανερώθητε ἡμῖν ὥσπερ ἀστέ-ρες ἐπαναστράπτοντες, σημεῖα καὶ τεράστια καὶ ἰαμάτων χαρίσματα, ἀθλοφόροι αὐτάδελφοι¹, τῶν Ἀγγέλων ὁμόσκηνοι.

That the martyrs should be stars might be explained from popular figures (such expressions being common enough in the Menaea), but that the two particular stars should be called a

¹ Note that this word in this connexion and in this literature often means δίδυμοι, especially such δίδυμοι as are sons of one mother but of different sires, like Castor and Pollux.

φωσφόρος ὄντως δυάς suggests that the Greek prayers and hymns have preserved for the saints the traces of their previous history as demigods. It is, however, quite possible that the parallels adduced may be conventional.

We have now traced Florus and Laurus to their origin in Pagan ritual. Our investigation has identified them with some form of the cult of the great twin-brethren. We assumed that these were Castor and Pollux, but it must be remembered that the twin-brethren turn up under various names. They might have been, for instance, Amphion and Zethus. If we had started from these, the argument would have been strengthened, as regards the recognition of the Twins as builders, as the following considerations will show.

We have alluded to the variety of forms in which the cult of the twin-brethren existed; and this variety will be sure to be reflected upon the cult of the saints that replace them. There must be an adaptation of the displacing religion to that which is displaced. It is not likely that the same saints would replace the pair Castor-Polydeuces, and the pair Amphion-Zethus: and even when we allow for the general assimilation of the different forms in which the Twins were worshipped locally, there will still be enough variety in their names and in their ritual to ensure a corresponding variety in the calendar.

Now, with regard to Amphion and Zethus, we have reason to believe that they are the Dioscuri of Thebes. We are told by John Malala, that amongst the architectural gifts of the Emperor Tiberius to the city of Antioch, there were two monuments which were set up in honour of the Dioscuri sprung from Antiope whose names are Amphion and Zethus. We shall have occasion to refer again to this important tradition which Malala has preserved; for the present we simply quote it to show that the very term Dioscuri was applicable to Amphion and Zethus. And although their names do not seem to betray relationship, it is well known that they are twins from one mother. The parallel with the Dioscuri of Sparta at this point is very close; for here also the paternity is divided and the pair is a conjunction of mortal and immortal. In

some verses which Pausanias quotes from the poet Asius we
are told :

And Antiope bore Zethus and divine Amphion,
She the daughter of Asopus, the deep-eddying river,
Having conceived by Zeus and by Epopeus, shepherd of peoples.

Here Amphion is evidently of a higher birth than Zethus :
and this tradition appears to have been widely accepted.

We observe further that the Theban twins are horsemen,
like those of Sparta. The word used to describe them is
λευκόπωλος: it is the same word which Sophocles *Ajax* 673
uses to describe the 'white-steeds of the morning'':

ἐξίσταται δὲ νυκτὸς αἰανῆς κύκλος
τῇ λευκοπώλῳ φέγγος ἡμέρᾳ φλέγειν.

Thus also in Euripides' *Phoenissae* 606, Thebes, the home
of Amphion and Zethus, is spoken of as

θεῶν τῶν λευκοπώλων δώματα,

and in Euripides, *Hercules Furens* 29, 30, they are similarly
described :

τὼ λευκοπώλω πρὶν τυραννῆσαι χθονὸς
'Αμφίον' ἠδὲ Ζῆθον ἐκγόνω Διός.

The language suggests that they are connected with the
daybreak, in the same way as Castor and his brother : though
the daystar does not shine so clearly on the Theban heads as
on the Spartan. Further, they are builders; this was a point
to which we were led, in identifying Florus and Laurus with
the Dioscuri : the evidence is more abundant for the Theban
twins. Not only have we the rich and varied tradition of their
building the walls of Thebes, but we find other local references
of a similar character.

Before they built Thebes, they are said to have walled a
city whose name is Eutresis. According to Strabo, IX. p. 411,

Εὔτρησιν κωμίον Θεσπιέων· ἐνταῦθά φασι Ζῆθον καὶ 'Αμφίονα οἰκῆσαι πρὶν
βασιλεῦσαι Θηβῶν.

The same tradition appears in Stephanus of Byzantium :

Εὔτρησις ἦν ἐτείχισε Ζῆθος καὶ 'Αμφίων· ἐκλήθη δὲ Εὔτρησις διὰ τὸ
πολλαῖς αὐτὴν πρότερον χρῆσασθαι ῥύμαις, ὡς 'Επαφρόδιτος.

There is also a curious tradition (perhaps a direct Theban migration) that they were also the builders of Dyrrachium: cf. Anna Comnena, *Alexiad* III. p. 99 D,

ἐν ὑστέροις δὲ χρόνοις (ὡς "Ελληνές φασι καὶ αὐτὰ δὴ τὰ ἐν τῇ πόλει γλυπτὰ γράμματα μαρτυροῦσιν) ὑπ' 'Αμφίονος καὶ Ζήθου ἀνοικοδομηθεῖσα εἰς ὃ νῦν ὁρᾶται σχῆμα. αὐτίκα δὲ τὴν κλῆσιν μεταμείψασα Δυρράχιον προσηγορεύεται.

Thus the evidence that the Theban twins were builders with stone is quite conclusive, and the result is a confirmation of the correctness of our interpretation of the meaning of the occupation of Florus and Laurus.

We have sufficiently established the parallelism between the Theban twins and those of Sparta. The final decision as to which pair immediately precedes Florus and Laurus we leave undecided. Nor have we found the reason for the names of the new objects of worship. According to Albert the twins are represented on a vase from Vulci, along with Leda who holds in her right hand a flower and in her left two branches of laurel. Perhaps this may throw light on it.

CHAPTER II.

JUDAS THOMAS.

WE now pass on to examine another case of Christian
hagiology which appears to reflect the story of the Dioscuri.
We may recognize at once that the following principles
should guide us in such investigations; first, that if the worship
of the Dioscuri were the same wherever the cult existed, we
should not be entitled to assume that the cult would be displaced everywhere in the same manner. There may be more
ways than one of getting rid of the Dioscuri, and besides
Florus and Laurus, we may stumble upon other pairs of twins
who are their equivalents. And second, that since there is
every reason to believe that the worship of the Dioscuri was
the survival of a series of local cults, competing *inter se* for
honours and preëminence, we have an additional reason for
expecting variety in the displacement of the cults when they
ceased to be Pagan and became Christian.

In looking over the calendar for possible local cults of the
twin-brethren, there is one case of supreme interest which
attracts our attention.

In the city of Edessa, as is well known, the leading saint
is S. Thomas the Apostle, and it is universally conceded that
S. Thomas is somebody's twin-brother. It is not, however, so
commonly recognized that, in Edessa, the definition of the twin-
brother had been made in a manner sufficiently startling to
modern ears, and that S. Thomas was regarded as the twin of
Christ. The proof of this lies, in the first instance, in a study
of that remarkable apocryphal work the Acts of Thomas, from

whose fantastic pages we constantly see, starting up before our eyes, the expression 'twin of the Messiah,' although the term is sometimes disguised by feeble corrections of the term Thomas into *Tehoma, the abyss* or *the ocean-flood*[1]. In fact, to the Syrian Church in early times, Thomas was not a name at all; he was Judas Thomas, i.e. Jude the [Lord's] twin-brother. The confusion is one which can be traced in the oldest copies of the Syriac Gospel, and in the earliest literature of the Eastern Church. (Cf. the Lewis Syriac in John xiv. 22 for the identification of Judas and Thomas.) The writer of the Acts (which, as a study of their language will show, are originally Syriac, and not a translation), has evidently made the assumed relation of the twin-brethren in his story one of the leading motives in his romance; Jesus is constantly mistaken for Judas his twin, and Judas for Jesus. They are perfectly alike; and it is not surprising that the pious people in the story, as well as the impious, are constantly deceived.

Without going into detail, at the present time, either as to the peculiar Edessan idea, or as to the way in which it was reflected on the apocryphal Acts or on the rest of the literature of the Church, we will, for the sake of illustration, give one or two of the statements in the Acts upon which we have based the foregoing remarks, reserving the complete treatment of the subject for another occasion[2].

For example, one of the stories which make up the Acta Thomae is a tale of an ass's colt which, at the commandment of Judas Thomas, opened its mouth and spoke:

(Ed. Wright, p. 179.) And the mouth of the colt was opened, and it spake like a man by the power of our Lord, and said to him, '*Twin of the Christ*,' &c.[3]

---

[1] E.g. Wright, p. 170 (the speech of the Black Snake), "I do not dare to utter these things because I know that the Ocean Flood (*lege*, the Twin) of the Messiah will destroy our nature."

[2] Mr Burkitt has drawn attention to the matter in the *Journal of Theological Studies*, I. 288. My investigations are entirely independent, and the results were obtained, for the most part, some years ago. I am glad to have the corroboration of his careful study.

[3] Here the Syriac has made an attempt to correct ܬܐܘܡܐ ('twin of') into ܬܗܘܡܐ ('ocean-flood of'), evidently with the view of softening the

and the likeness of Judas to Jesus comes out in such passages as the following from the *Story of a Demon that dwelt in a Woman* (Wright, p. 185). The demon says, 'What have we to do with thee, Apostle of the Most High?... *Why art thou like unto God thy Lord*, who concealed His majesty and appeared in the flesh?...For thou, namely, art born of Him.' Thus the Syriac, but a reference to the Greek shows a much stronger text:

τίνος ἕνεκα ἐξομοιοῦσαι τῷ υἱῷ τοῦ Θεοῦ τῷ ἀδικήσαντι ἡμᾶς; ἔοικας γὰρ ἑαυτῷ πάνυ ὡς ἐξ αὐτοῦ ἀποκυηθείς.

Judas, that is to say, is as like to His Lord as if he had been begotten of Him. There is much more of the same kind in the Acta. These statements are emphatic and repeated throughout the book, and they show that the writer not only held a current Edessan belief as to the twin-ship of Jesus and Judas, but that *he made it one of the main threads of his argument, and the leading motive of his fancy.*

In certain Edessan circles, then, whether Christian or Gnostic, a peculiar belief was current as to the twin who occurs in the table of the Twelve Apostles. And in such circles, and in the mind of the writer of the Acts of Thomas, we have to allow that Jesus and Judas stood for a pair of twin-brethren, one of them being presumed to be mortal and the other immortal, if we may argue from the nature of the case and the parallel with the Dioscuri.

And the question arises naturally whether, as we have found the motive of the likeness between Jesus and Judas running through the Acta, we ought not to find that the legends of the Dioscuri have been imitated, or at all events have affected the invention of the religious novelist to whom we owe the apocryphal work in question.

text. But the Greek of the passage is quite decided, as the following will show:

Acta Thomae (ed. 1, Bonnet, p. 29, ed. 2, p. 156). τοῦ δὲ ἀποστόλου ἔτι ἑστῶτος ἐν τῇ λεωφόρῳ καὶ διαλεγομένου τῷ πλήθει πῶλος ὀνάδος ἦλθεν καὶ ἔστη ἔμπροσθεν αὐτοῦ καὶ ἀνοίξας τὸ στόμα αὐτοῦ εἶπεν· Ὁ δίδυμος τοῦ Χριστοῦ, ὁ ἀπόστολος τοῦ Χριστοῦ κτέ.

The story opens, as is well known, with the sale of Judas Thomas by Jesus to a merchant named Ḥabban who is going to India. The purchase having been completed, Ḥabban says to Judas, 'What is thy art which thou art skilled in practising?' Judas saith to him, 'Carpentering and architecture—the business of the carpenter.' Ḥabban the merchant saith to him, 'What dost thou know to make in wood and what in hewn stone?' Judas saith to him, 'In wood I have learned to make ploughs and yokes and ox-goads and oars for ferry-boats, and masts for ships: and in stone, tombstones and monuments and temples and palaces for kings.' Ḥabban is very pleased with the qualifications of his new slave, and so they set sail.

Notice how the Christian apostle is introduced as one who can make stone temples[1]: and recall what we found out with regard to the Dioscuri in the south of the Peloponnesus, and with regard to Florus and Laurus in Illyricum.

On the journey to India, Ḥabban and his new slave put in at the city Sandaruk, where they happen to come at a festive season, for it is the marriage of the king's daughter. At the feast which the king gives certain miracles are wrought by Judas, which result in his being carried off into the bride-chamber *that he may pray for a blessing upon the young people*. After Judas has prayed, he leaves the bride-chamber, and in a little while our Lord appears to the bride and bridegroom, who promptly take him for Judas, which evokes the explanation, 'I am not Judas, but I am the brother of Judas.' The rest of the story must be read in the Acts of Thomas. But we have not gone so far without recognizing that the appearance of the twin-brethren in the bride-chamber is borrowed from current ideas as to the blessings bestowed on newly-married people by the Dioscuri[2].

---

[1] The 'ploughs and yokes' might conceivably have come from the tradition of the occupation of Jesus, given by Justin. But this source will not do for the temples.

[2] It is said that the Dioscuri exercised similar influences at Roman weddings. See Myriantheus, *Die Açvins*, p. 118, quoting Rossbach, *Römische Grabdenkmäler*. In the same connexion we may recall the Roman deities Mutunus and Tutunus, who preside over sexual intercourse. Their names suggest twins; and they are probably a very early form of the cult of the Twins in Italy, which has been

The incident of the wedding being over (which must have been deliberately introduced by the artist, for there was no need for the travellers to disembark when the main action is evidently to be in India) they proceed on their journey, and arrive at last at the kingdom of Gondafar.

And now begins the second Act, when Thomas the Apostle entered into India and built a palace for the king in heaven. Habban brings Judas before the king, who engages him to build a new palace, supplying him with abundance of gold and silver. All of this Judas promptly puts in circulation as alms to the poor. He went about and ministered and made many afflicted persons comfortable. The king kept on sending money, and Judas kept on spending it, a process which was of necessity terminable as soon as information reached the king.

We need hardly point out how close is the parallel at this point with the story of Florus and Laurus, who spend the money that is given them on the poor, working all day on the temple and praying all night, until Licinius the governor finds them out.

In the Acts of Thomas, when the fraud is discovered the king resolves that he will burn Judas, after first flaying him, along with Habban the merchant; he is, however, dissuaded by the spirit of his brother who dies, comes to life again and reports that he has seen the palace in heaven which Judas had built.

In the Florus and Laurus legend, we are told that Licinius

preserved amongst that most conservative people the Romans. See Tert. *Adv. Nat.* ii. 11, Arnob. *Adv. Nat.* iv. 11.

Another similar pair are Pilumnus and Picumnus, who are described by Varro as 'dii conjugales' and 'dii infantium,' see Nonius Marcellus, p. 528. 13 and Servius on Verg. *Aen.* x. 76.

The following is the description of Picumnus and Pilumnus given in Petiscus' *Gods of Olympos* (Eng. tr. p. 156).

"Picumnus and Pilumnus were a pair of brother gods who presided over marriage. When a child was born, a couch was prepared in the house for Picumnus, for he, as god of agriculture, could ensure health and wealth. Pilumnus with his club (*pilum*), the instrument with which he threshed the corn, warded off all evil influence from the newborn babe. These two brothers had done many doughty deeds in peace and war, *and were often compared with the Dioscuri, Castor and Pollux.*"

burnt alive all the poor people who had taken money from the Twins, and then he bound the brethren to a wheel and flayed them.

We are evidently dealing with parallel streams of folk-lore: and if we go outside the Syriac Acts into the general body of the Thomas legends, the parallels are even more striking. For example, let us turn to the Ethiopic literature. Here we find in the *Contendings of the Apostles* which Budge has published, not only an Ethiopic version of the Acts of Thomas but also a parallel set of legends, called the *Preaching of S. Thomas in India.*

As in the ordinary legend, Thomas is sold for a slave to Arbasos, an officer of king Kontaros. The qualifications of the slave are given, much as in the Acta, plus the additional one that Judas can act as a physician (like the Açvius in Indian mythology) and can heal the wounds that work decay in the flesh. He is accordingly brought before the king, and the king sends him to Lukyanos or Lukiyos the governor, with instructions to supply him with everything that he needs (note the name of the governor and compare with Lycon and Licinius in the Florus and Laurus legend).

Now let us see what happens when Thomas spends his building money on the poor.

And Lukiyos said unto him in wrath, ' O thou wicked slave, where is the fulfilment of the word which thou didst speak unto me ? ' Then he commanded them to put Thomas in prison and they stretched him out there. And *they made a wheel* in the ground and bound him upon it, and Lukiyos commanded the executioners *to strip the skin from his body.*

The parallels with the Florus and Laurus legend are even more pronounced in the Ethiopic legend than in the Syriac.

The story goes on to say that Thomas was healed by our Lord, and that he went about working miracles by means of his skin which he carried with him as an aegis. Lukiyos was converted and set over the new church that was formed.

I have, however, found no parallel in the Thomas legends to the throwing of Florus and Laurus into a well.

But we are not yet at the end of the suggestive parallels between the Thomas legends and the Dioscuri. In the Rig-

veda horses and chariots occur constantly, but there is no
mention of the ass except in connexion with the Açvins, who
clearly are ass-drivers and ass-tamers as well as horsemen ; and
in the Thomas legends there are two stories in which the ass
finds a prominent place, and one of them is an actual case of
ass-taming.　According to Macdonnell[1], "the Açvins' name
implies only the possession of horses, there being no evidence
to show that they are so called because they ride on them....In
the *Aitareya Brahmana* the Açvins are said at the marriage
of Soma and Sūryā to have won a race in a car drawn by asses."
This makes them ὀνόδαμοι as well as ἱππόδαμοι.　They are
also said to drive asses in their chariot in the morning twilight[2].
Now in the Acts of Thomas a whole section is devoted to the
miraculous taming of a team of wild asses.　The general of
king Mazdai drives Judas in his chariot to pay a healing visit
to his wife and daughter.　[Compare the deliverance of Sūryā
the daughter of the Sun by the Açvins and the rescue of Helen
by the Dioscuri.]　In such a connexion there was no reason to
make the chariot break down : it is an incident deliberately
introduced; and the only conceivable reason for its introduction
is that the legends of the Dioscuri may be imitated who, at the
close of the day, change from a team of bright horses to a team
of gray asses, and that Judas may show, like the Twins, his
power of taming and driving the wild asses.　When the carriage
horses are worn out with the journey, and refuse to move
further, Judas summons a team of four wild asses from a herd,
and finishes the journey with them: 'the wild asses going
along gently and quietly and by little and little, that the
Apostle of God might not be shaken.'　And the colour of the
incident is Vedic and early Greek in this respect, that the
riding is done in a chariot, and the animals are broken in to
drive[3].

---

[1] *Vedic Mythology*, p. 49.

[2] See Myriantheus, pp. 74, 103. Myriantheus acutely suggests that the
appearance of asses in the chariot of the Açvins where we have ordinarily the
red and white horses, is an attempt to express the colour of the sky, whose
morning-gray is the colour of the ass.

[3] This does not apply to the other story of the ass colt on which Judas
is persuaded to ride a little way.

Another striking feature shall be mentioned, connecting the Thomas legends with those of the Dioscuri. When Judas has converted a great many people to the faith, it becomes necessary for him to set some one over them ecclesiastically, that the flock may be properly shepherded. For this purpose he selects his deacon Xanthippus[1]. The name is peculiar, in view of the general prevalence of Persian and Indian names in the legend. But there would be no need to draw attention to the introduction of a Greek name, any more than in the case of the Latin name Tertia which occurs later on, if it were not that Xanthippos is so nearly the name of one of the horses in the team driven by the Dioscuri. More exactly the names of the horses presented by Hera to the Twins are *Xanthos* and Kyllaros[2].

The name Xanthippos appears to me to indicate, not only that the writer of the Acta had the Dioscuri and their legends in mind, but that he knew these legends in their Greek form. And it should be noticed that this account of Xanthippos[3] occurs in the very same part of the legends that is devoted to the taming of the wild asses. Nor should we omit one other feature which is adumbrated, without any special treatment being devoted to it, in the same section. In making his farewell address to the new converts, Judas commends them to the power of Christ who is able to preserve them waking and

---

[1] The Greek translator was puzzled over the name, which looks oddly enough in Syriac, and transcribed it Xenophon!

[2] According to Roscher, *Lex.* I. 1156, " Ihren Rossen gab die Poesie Namen, Xanthos (ein sehr gewöhnlicher Pferdename) und Kyllaros (auch Name von Kentauren). Diese beiden sollte Hera gegeben haben, die sie von Poseidon hatte."

[3] The thought suggests itself that the charioteers of the Twins may have actually been named Xanthippus and Leucippus in some one of the traditions concerning them. But I have not succeeded in verifying this. According to Strabo (XI. 2. 12) the Spartans founded in Colchis the colony of Heniochia ('Hνιοχία) under the leadership of Rhecas and Amphistratos the charioteers of the Dioscuri, the colonists being known as the Heniochi or charioteers. But there are other variant forms of the names. In Ammianus Marcellinus (xx. 8. 24) we have Amphitos and Cercios, instead of Amphistratos and Rhecas (" et Dioscurias nunc usque nota cuius auctores Amphitus et Cercius Spartani traduntur, aurigae Castoris et Pollucis, quibus Heniochorum natio est instituta "). The language shows that this is the same tradition as occurs in Strabo.

sleeping: "and if," says he, "*ye sit in a ship and on the sea*
where no man of you is able to help his fellow, He will walk
upon the waves of the sea and support your ship[1]." It need
hardly be pointed out how closely this reflects the sailors' view
of the Dioscuri.   It is introduced abruptly, and addressed
apparently to a non-seafaring people: the reason for its introduction lies in the Vedic and Greek parallels, where the
Dioscuri walk on the sea to save their worshippers.

Upon the whole, then, we conclude that the writer of the
Acts of Judas Thomas has for his raw material the Acts of the
Dioscuri, and just as these underlie the legends of Florus and
Laurus in Illyricum, so they also underlie the apocryphal
stories of Edessa.

The next question which presents itself to the mind, in
connexion with the recognition of the influence which the
legends of the Dioscuri are here held to have exercised over
the legends of S. Thomas, relates to the underlying assumption
that the cult of the Dioscuri was known and practised in the
city of Edessa.   That the Acts of Thomas were actually written
in Edessa is highly probable.   It is practically admitted in the
Syriac Acts, as we possess them, by the concluding statements
as to the conveyance of the relics of S. Thomas from India to
the West.   Historical and geographical locations of bones that
work miracles are usually made by people who claim to possess
them.   Then we have the Bardesan hymns inserted in the text,
or at least one of them; and other Edessan features can probably
be recognized.   But why should the Dioscuri have prominence
in Edessa?   And if an Edessan writer has his mind so full of
the legends of the Twins that he imitates them in a series of
Acts of certain other twins, are we not obliged to infer that he
was actually displacing a cult, and not merely amusing himself
by the adaptation of a piece of folk-lore to a fresh literary
statement?   The answer to this enquiry ought, I think, to be
in the affirmative.   We have almost a right to expect that the
Dioscuri in some form or other were worshipped at Edessa.

---

[1] Cf. Myriantheus, p. 158.   "Bravely did you bear yourselves on the sea,
where there is no support nor aught that a man can hold to, when ye brought
Bhuyyu home, who stood on the ship with a hundred oars."

But how is this to be demonstrated or at all events to be made probable?

Every one who has visited Ourfa (Edessa), that city of saints, scholars and martyrs, will remember its most conspicuous feature, the two colossal pillars which rise skyward from its citadel, and which are unitedly known to the native population as the Throne of Nimrod. Of these twin pillars the more southerly is inscribed in archaic Syriac characters, near the middle of the column, with a statement that some one, whose name has not been deciphered, made this pillar and a statue for Queen Shalmath, the daughter of Ma'nu. The statues, for we should probably read the word in the plural, have disappeared, though they might very likely be recovered by excavation round the base of the pillars on which they once stood. According to Sachau[1] following the chronicle of Edessa, the citadel was built in A.D. 206 under Abgar VIII. (Severus bar Ma'nu) who reigned from 176—213: and the pillars may, if of later date than the citadel, have been erected under Abgar VIII. or his successor Abgar IX. (Ma'nu), the last of the princes of Edessa. But Sachau is disposed to think it possible that the pillars were there long before Abgar VIII. built (or re-built) the citadel. What then are these pillars? *In my judgment they are representative of or votive to the great twin-brethren.* For it should be observed that neither in the inscription nor on the pillars is there any sign of Christianity: and we have, therefore, to look for a cult in which two such pillars would be a proper emblem[2].

---

[1] *Edessenische Inschriften.*

[2] The pillars at Edessa are evidently similar in the intention of worship, and in outward appearance, to the pillars which stood in the great temple at Hierapolis (Mabbog), described by Lucian in *De Syria Dea*. It has been the custom to give these latter pillars a naturalistic meaning; and it may be asked whether, if such a meaning be proper in Hierapolis, we ought to attach any further or other meaning to the neighbouring pair in Edessa. The circumstances are so like, that the hypotheses explaining the circumstances ought to be similar also. There is some force in this reasoning. It seems, however, to have been forgotten that in both cases we have not only to explain the raising of a votive pillar of unusual height, but of *a pair* of such pillars. Any explanation which ignores that the pillars are pairs, fails to explain them adequately. And this means that the naturalistic hypothesis is insufficient. The only

At this point there comes to our aid the tradition which John Malala preserved concerning the city of Antioch[1], and its decoration by the Emperor Tiberius. The language of Malala is as follows (p. 234):

Ἔκτισε δὲ καὶ ἱερὸν τῷ Διονύσῳ πρὸς τῷ ὄρει ὁ αὐτὸς Τιβέριος βασιλεύς, στήσας δύο στήλας μεγάλας τῶν ἐξ Ἀντιόπης γεννηθέντων Διοσκούρων ἔξω τοῦ ναοῦ εἰς τιμὴν αὐτῶν, Ἀμφίονος τε καὶ Ζήθου.

Here is a case of the erection of twin-monuments which is exactly parallel to the lofty twin-pillars of Hierapolis and of Edessa: and this time the explanation of the cult is given: the columns are in honour of the Dioscuri: and I do not think we need to hesitate, in view of the Malala tradition, to say that we have found the meaning of the columns at Edessa[2].

It is unfortunate that this Edessan inscription is so difficult to decipher on account of its altitude and the paucity of long

direction in which I see how to throw light upon the structures is to introduce either (i) the Dioscuri or (ii) the Kabiri (Μεγάλοι Θεοί). But since these two explanations are separated by a very narrow gulf, and the titles, functions and artistic representations of the brethren very nearly tally with one another, it is hardly worth while introducing the Kabiri. So the real question is whether the Dioscuri have a naturalistic interpretation sufficiently pronounced to meet the description in Lucian. By the way, Lucian will have it that the pillars at Mabbog were an actual dedication to Hera by Dionysos, and he gives the inscription. It must be fictitious or misread. Compare the Edessan inscription.

[1] For earlier traces of the Dioscuri at Antioch we can go back to the coins of Seleucus Nicator. See Babelon, *Inventaire de la Collection Waddington.*

[2] It is possible that Nisibis also had the same architectural appointment, for its name means simply The Columns. The present town of Nisibin has little remaining of its former splendour; a few columns are still standing, probably from some ancient building. Badger says two columns, which Sachau corrects to five. It is not likely that these surviving pillars have anything to do with the name of the city or with the Dioscuri. It is worth noting, in passing, that the writer of the Acts of Thomas knows Nisibis. Its Roman name is *Mygdonia* or rather *Antioch in Mygdonia*: and this is the name which is given in the Acts to the wife of the kinsman of King Mazdai. Accordingly we are told that ' a woman, the wife of the king's kinsman, her name was Mygdonia, had come to see the new sight of the new God who was preached.' Is this an allegorical way of describing the conversion of Nisibis?

There was also a temple of the Dioscuri at Seleucia, the port of Antioch, as we learn from Polybius (*Hist.* v. 60. 4). But that is natural enough; the case is the same as at Ostia, which also had one.

ladders in Ourfa. There seems to be no doubt as to the name of the queen, Shalmath daughter of Ma'nu. It is justified to some extent by the Doctrine of Addai, where Shalmath the princess appears as the daughter of Meherdates and the niece of Abgar the Black.

I do not like to abandon the inscription without a further attempt at deciphering its object and intention. The transcription of it, so far as I personally attempted it in 1896, did not furnish anything beyond what had already been attained by Sachau in his *Edessenische Inschriften*, and I shall therefore use Sachau's readings and comments.

The crux of the inscription does not lie in the opening lines, which contain the name of the person who set up the pillars, but in the word which follows the description of 'pillars and statue[s]' and precedes the name of 'Shalmath the queen, the daughter of Ma'nu.' The reading of Sachau is as follows:

Z. 5.   ܡܠܟܬܐ ܟܘܪܣܝܐܘ oder ܟܘܪܣܠܟ.   Ob zu lesen ist

ܟܘܪܣܝܐܘ ܕܨܠܡܬܗ ?

and in accordance with this speculation he translates,

diese Säule und Statue, das Bildniss der Shalmath.

Now I am extremely sceptical about this interpretation, which makes the statue to be an image of Shalmath herself. There is no need to add a word after 'Statue,' if Shalmath is meant; moreover the reading should be 'for Shalmath,' in which case it is some other person's image or statue. At the same time I suspect that Sachau is right in conjecturing that the word which perplexed him is ܨܠܡܬܗ or something very like it.

Suppose we turn to Land, *Anecdota Syriaca* I. 32, where we shall find a list of the signs of the Zodiac, as they were current in Edessa in the days immediately after Bardesanes, that is, at the very time when our pillars were erected. We are told, apparently on the authority of Sergius of Res'aina, that "these are the names of the signs of the Zodiac according to the house of Bardesan." The list is reprinted by Nöldeke in ZDMG. 25. 256, with some corrections, and with the parallel lists from

Bar Hebraeus and from the Mandaean literature; it runs as follows:

	Syriac	*Mandaean*
Aries	ܐܡܪܐ	ܐܡܒܪܐ
Taurus	ܬܘܪܐ	ܬܐܘܪܐ
Gemini	ܬܪܝܢ ܨܠܡ̈ܐ (Bar Heb. ܬܐܡ̈ܐ)	ܨܠܡ̈ܐ
Cancer	ܣܪܛܢܐ	ܣܐܪܛܐܢܐ
Leo	ܐܪܝܐ	ܐܪܝܐ
Virgo	ܒܬܘܠܬܐ	ܫܘܡܒܘܠܬܐ
Libra	ܡܘܙܢܝܐ (Bar Heb. ܡܣܐܬܐ)	ܩܐܢܐ
Scorpius	ܥܩܪܒܐ	(sic ?) ܐܩܪܒܐ
Arcitenens	ܨܠܡܐ ܪܒܐ (Bar Heb. ܩܫܬܐ)	ܢܐܛܩܐ
Caper	ܓܕܝܐ	ܐܓܕܝܐ
Amphora	ܕܘܠܐ	ܕܐܘܠܐ
Pisces	ܢܘܢܐ	ܢܘܢܐ

Now here we notice that two of the signs, namely Gemini and Sagittarius, are described as 'figures,' the former being the 'two figures,' the latter the 'great figure.' For the description 'two figures' Bar Hebraeus restores the conventional 'twins'; for the 'great figure' Bar Hebraeus gives 'the archer,' while the Mandaean means either 'bow' or 'arrow.' The variation shows that the name 'great figure' was not very stable; it was likely to be replaced. The name for Gemini is a better established one; for although Bar Hebraeus has replaced it in his list by 'Twins,' in his Chronicon he speaks of 'Mercury being in conjunction with the two figures' (ܐܪܡܣ ܒܬܪܝܢ ܨܠܡ̈ܐ ܐܬܬܐܡ). We should compare the Indian names of the signs of the Zodiac, where Gemini = two faces, and Sagittarius = arrow. The Edessan list is half-way to India.

Now it seems to me that we should read in the inscription some form like that suggested by Sachau, and interpret it in the sense suggested by the Bardesanian lists of the signs of the Zodiac, viz.

the pillar and the statue of the Figures (i.e. of the Twins) for Shalmath the queen, the daughter of Ma'nu.

The exact form of the restored word is not quite certain; but it was probably very near to the Mandaean ܟ̈ܠܐܒܐ. It seems to have been a little longer than the Syriac plural ܟ̈ܠܐ; not ܨܠܡܗ (her image), but perhaps ܟܠܐܒ.

We may, I think, conclude that the sign of the Dioscuri was in the inscription, and that the road by which we have come to the conclusion was a correct one. The twin pillars were, like the Antioch monuments, dedicated to the Twins, whose Bardesanian name, or some close approximation to it, was actually inscribed.

But we have now taken the enquiry to a further point: we have not only shown that the worship of the Dioscuri must have been popular in Edessa, but we have almost connected it officially with the royal house. And it becomes proper to ask whether there are any confirmations of the correctness of this view from the Syriac literature or from the numismatics of the country.

The names of the ruling princes do not, I think, show any trace of the influence of the Dioscuri. There are indications of solar worship. For instance, the mausoleum of one of the princesses of the Abgar dynasty shows in Greek and in Syriac the name of Amassamses ('Amath Shemesh). Here we have the name 'Solar Handmaid' in the royal family, and a prevalent form of worship is betrayed thereby. We have also the testimony of Julian that Edessa had been from time immemorial a centre of sun worship (ἱερὸν ἐξ αἰῶνος ἡλίου χωρίον)[1]. But solar worship does not necessarily involve the cult of the Dioscuri.

When we turn to the coins of the Abgar dynasty we find amongst the moneys struck in Edessa a number of coins bearing signs, which must be held to have some non-Christian connotation: of these the chief are (i) a star, (ii) the crescent moon. Now the star, whether single or double, is the sign of the twin-brethren. Golden stars were offered in their honour in the temple at Delphi (see Plutarch, *Lysander* 18). According to Diodorus Siculus (IV. 43) the stars actually fell on the heads

---

[1] See also Duval, *Journal Asiatique* for 1891, p. 228.

of the Twins after a storm in the Black Sea. The star appears over their heads on coins: for a beautiful example from the coins of S. Italy (Bruttii) see Percy Gardner, *Types of Greek Coins*, Plate XI. 36, 38, where the Twins appear on both sides of a single coin, in each case surmounted by stars; the obverse shows them riding, the reverse gives their heads only, with the characteristic half-egg-shaped pilos. For another interesting example in the same volume, we may turn to Plate XIII. 10, which is described by Gardner as follows:

> On No. 10 from Berytus in Troas, is a young head wearing a conical pileus surmounted by a star. If we were guided by considerations of origin, we might probably see in it one of the Cabeiri of Samothrace, but in the days of rapid spread of Hellenism *the people of Troas would probably rather call it one of the Dioscuri.*

Many other instances may be found in Albert's *Castor et Pollux en Italie.*

If we turn to Babelon's account of the coinage of Edessa[1] we shall find all or most of the cases in which the star and the crescent are found. I give the numbers from Babelon's list.

No. 25.   A coin of Abgar VIII.: a star and a crescent on his tiara.

No. 26.   A coin of Abgar VIII. : three stars and a crescent on his tiara, one of the stars being within the crescent.

No. 27.   A coin of Abgar VIII. : two stars and a crescent on his tiara.

No. 28.   A coin of Abgar VIII. : two stars and a crescent on his tiara.

No. 29.   A coin of Abgar VIII.: three stars and a crescent on his tiara, as in No. 26.

No. 31.   A coin of Abgar VIII.: a single star on the tiara. All of these coins have the head of Septimius Severus on the other side.

No. 34.   A coin of Abgar VIII. and on the reverse the head of his son Ma'nu. Abgar's tiara has three stars and a crescent, as in No. 26.

No. 35.   A similar coin with a single star and a crescent. These two coins belong to the time of Caracalla.

No. 59.   A coin of Alexander Severus: on the reverse the Fortune of Edessa, with two stars.

No. 61.   A coin of Alexander Severus: on the reverse the Fortune of Edessa, with two stars.

---

[1] Published in *Revue de Numismatique Belge*, 1892 and 1893, and afterwards reprinted in his *Mélanges Numismatiques.*

No. 67. A coin of Alexander Severus : on the reverse the Fortune of Edessa, with two stars.

No. 79. A coin of Alexander Severus and Julia Mammaea: on the reverse the Fortune of Edessa, with four stars, two on each side of the figure.

No. 84. A coin of Julia Mammaea : on the reverse the Fortune of Edessa, with two stars.

No. 89. A coin of Gordian ; on the reverse the Fortune of Edessa, with two stars.

Nos. 96.⎫
    97.⎪ A coin of Gordian, with a star : on the reverse Abgar with a
    98.⎬   star.
    99.⎭

No. 100. A coin of Gordian : on the reverse Abgar with a star on his tiara.

From the foregoing instances (and no doubt others might be added), it is clear that the star and the crescent are common features of the Edessan coinage. The usual number of stars is two: in one case this is doubled, perhaps because there are two imperial heads on the coin. In certain other cases the stars are three, but one of them lies in the lunar crescent, and apparently belongs to it.

Now the crescent appearing with two stars turns up on coins of Asia Minor elsewhere ; for instance, on coins of Termessos and Akalisos in Lycia, and Kodrula in Pisidia. See Imhoof-Blumer, *Choix*, pl. 5, 172, *Monn. Gr.* p. 345. On these coins the Dioscuri appear with stars, accompanied by a female figure with a crescent. Imhoof-Blumer in *Choix* identified the female figure with Artemis, but in *Monn. Gr.* he says :

La femme placée entre le Dioscures, que M. Wieseler nomme Astarté, est Hélène, suivant M. Berndorf (*Arch. Zeit.* 1868, p. 39) et M. de Duhn (*Zeitschrift für Num.* III. p. 39).

No doubt this explanation of the figures is correct; and we propose to make a similar explanation of the stars and crescent upon the Edessa currency, in spite of the fact that we sometimes have an added star along with the crescent.

It is easy to see from the Parthian and Bactrian currencies how universal was the influence of Western types, and how

easily Western deities were identified with their parallels from
the Eastern mythologies. One of the most curious cases is
this very one of the Dioscuri, who come back to the Punjab
as mounted horsemen, and as such appear on the coins of
Eucratides[1].

So much for the coinage of Edessa, which is certainly not
unfavourable to the idea of the worship of the Twins in the
city. It is quite possible that Abgar himself may be posing as
one of the Dioscuri on his coins, as the Western emperors
frequently did.

We now turn to the literature to see if we can find any
traces of such worship. The first impression is discouraging,
for the pagan worship of which we know most in Edessa is the
survival of the worship of Bel and Nebo, the Assyrian deities.
And one would be disposed to say, at first sight, that this
must be the state religion. When, however, we turn to the
Doctrine of Addai[2], we find that Edessa was very eclectic, or
at least very varied, in its religious tastes. Accordingly Addai
says

I saw in this city that it abounded greatly in paganism, which is
against God. Who is this Nebo, an idol made which ye worship, and Bel,
whom ye honour? Behold, there are amongst you who adore Bath Nical,
as the inhabitants of Harran your neighbours, and Taratha, as the people
of Mabug, and the eagle, as the Arabians, also the sun and the moon,
as the rest of the inhabitants of Harran, who are as yourselves. *Be ye
not led away captive by the rays of the luminaries and the bright star*, for
every one who worships creatures is cursed before God.

The allusion to the worship of the 'splendid star' agrees
with the evidence of the Abgar coins; and Payne Smith shows
that the splendid star, ܟܘܟܒܐ, often stands for the planet
Venus, ὁ φωσφόρος.

There is no easy way to explain how the planet Venus
should appear double on the coins of Edessa, unless the stars
come there to represent the Dioscuri, who were originally

---

[1] Of this issue, Percy Gardner says (Pl. xiv. 23) "On No. 23 are the Dioscuri,
the Açvins of the Indians, charging on horseback, each bearing the palm of
victory."

[2] Ed. Phillips, p. 23.

the morning and evening star. I am disposed, therefore, to believe that the combined evidence of the two pillars in the citadel, and the frequent occurrence of the two stars on the coinage, is a sufficient ground for recognizing the worship of the Dioscuri in Edessa as a part of the state religion. It may be an original cult of the city revived under Western influences; but we do not seem to have sufficient evidence for tracing the matter further. We were led in search of such a cult, by the singular literary phenomenon furnished by the Acts of Thomas, where one pair of twins is evidently being ousted by another, and where the beneficent deeds of the Dioscuri are closely imitated: and we could hardly be wrong in assuming that the materials on which the artist was working, when he composed the Acts of Thomas, lay all around him. It is only in a community where the twin-brethren were honoured that such a work could have been produced. The hypothesis has found a certain amount of verification in what precedes, as far as the city of Edessa is concerned, and perhaps more may be forthcoming.

The road by which we arrived at our main conclusions is somewhat roundabout: we started with the curious fact of the displacement of the worship of the Dioscuri in Illyricum by the cult of a pair of stonemasons, and the transference of honours made it almost imperative that we recognized stone-craft amongst the arts of the Dioscuri.

We were led to consider certain parallel features in the Acts of Florus and Laurus and the Acts of Thomas, and especially the fact that Thomas also is at once a stonemason and a twin. On examining more closely the earliest traces of the worship of the Dioscuri in India, the hypothesis at once presented itself that the Acts of the Dioscuri underlay the Acts of Thomas, and that the necessary link was thus found for connecting together the scattered stories of Thomas's miracles. But this again made it necessary to assume that the worship of the Dioscuri must have prevailed in Edessa, as it did in Illyricum. Upon examination the confirmations were forthcoming.

If we had done nothing more than furnish an explanation

of the genesis of the perplexing Acts of Thomas, it would have been worth while. I have for years been seeking for some such elucidation. At first I thought that the key was the transference of some stories of Buddha and his disciples into the Christian legends. Moreover there were folk-lore parallels, especially in North-Western India, to some of the incidents in the Acta Thomae: for instance the story of the snake that sucks out his own poison and swells and bursts is genuine folk-lore. But what was my main obstacle in the enquiry was the fact that Thomas in the legends appears on the scenes as a builder in stone, and it did not seem that any such action could be predicated of Buddha or his disciples.

For as Count Goblet d'Alviella says[1],

Les écrivains classiques s'accordent à dire qu'à l'époque où Alexandre pénétra dans l'Inde, celle-ci ne possédait pas encore de bâtisses en pierre.

That single sentence was promptly entered on my Acts of Thomas as a warning against looking in the direction of *early Buddhism* for the stories in the Thomas legends. And the discouragement was effective. The matter was put aside, and I did not think of examining further into it; but by the time the unsuccessful speculation was forgotten, a similar difficulty arose with Florus and Laurus, who seemed to depend upon traditions of the Dioscuri as workers in stone, a thing of which the Rig-veda knows nothing. Fortunately the Dioscuri could not so easily be pushed aside, and an examination of their deeds and powers in Indian literature furnished the necessary ground for establishing the growth and development of the legends of the Dioscuri, as the cult moved westward, and finally for tracing their personalities behind the figures of Christ and His apostle in the Edessan legend.

All readers of the Acts of Thomas must have been struck with the difficulty of co-ordinating the incidents, and finding the string upon which the legends are arranged. The key, as in so many similar cases, is found by watching for the recurrent ideas: of these the first and foremost is that Jesus and Judas are twins: this is brought out, either by definite statements or

---

[1] *Ce que l'Inde doit à la Grèce*, p. 42.

by allusions to their likeness or optical equivalence, in every part of the book. The mistakes which are made in the identification, as the two leading figures interchange, are sufficient proof of what was uppermost in the writer's mind. When this is recognized, the next step in the unifying of the otherwise disperse collection of legends is by recognizing that the twins of the Acta Thomae are imitating other twins of whom popular religion had a great deal to say. When this is brought out, much that seems obscure or unnecessary in the Acta becomes significant. A hypothesis which connects together such remote and fantastic incidents as the introduction of Judas Thomas into the bride-chamber and the driving of a chariot drawn by wild asses on the way to rescue the wife and daughter of a general can hardly be destitute of literary validity.

But then, if this be correct, we have done something more than explain the literary genesis of the Acta Thomae; we have found out also the reason why Thomas is the apostle of Edessa; for the ecclesiastical situation is the same as that of Florus and Laurus in Illyricum. S. Thomas comes to displace non-S.-Thomas; a twin to eject twins, that is all; and no ecclesiastical history is made by his appearance in Ourfa, any more than by the appearance of other pairs of twins of the Castor-and-Pollux order elsewhere. To this an objection may be raised in the following form. We have the tradition from the Acta (if not from elsewhere) of the preaching of Thomas in India. Now it is noteworthy that the Acta do not place the preaching of Thomas in Edessa, though they bring his relics back thither. Why should Thomas go to India, when, on the hypothesis of the literary creation of the legend, he was wanted in Edessa? And even if we grant, what Mr Milne Rae has so admirably worked out in his study of the Syrian Church in India, that the preaching of S. Thomas in India is a case of the migration of traditions with the migrating Nestorians, still the migrating traditions must have started somewhere, and if not from Edessa, whence can they conceivably have come?

To these enquiries the answer lies in the following direction. The fact from which all the legends proceed is the displace-

ment of the cult of the twin-brethren in Edessa by a cult of
Jesus and Thomas. But this fact, which we have shown to be
the underlying motive of the Acta, opened up the way for a
second literary creation by the side of the one which we have
been studying. We have shown that the Zodiac of Edessa is in
some respects an Indian Zodiac. In the Indian Zodiac, the
Gemini are the first sign : and when the astrological problem
comes up, as to what countries are under the rule of particular
signs of the Zodiac, *India is assigned to the Twins.* Let us
think for a moment of this astrological fact, and see what
Christian problem is associated with it.

If we turn to the article on the Zodiac in the *Encyclopaedia
Britannica,* we shall find the following statement :

> The influence of the signs, though secondary, was overmastering :
> Julian called them θεῶν δυνάμεις, and they were the objects of a corre-
> sponding veneration. Cities and kingdoms were allotted to their several
> patronage on a system fully expounded by Manilius :
>
> > Hos erit in fines orbis pontusque notandus,
> > Quem Deus in partes per singula dividit astra,
> > Ac sua cuique dedit tutelae regna per orbem
> > Et proprias gentes atque urbes addidit altas,
> > In quibus exercent praestantia sidera vires.
>
> Manil. Astron. IV. 696.
>
> Syria was assigned to Aries, and Syrian coins frequently bear the image
> of a ram : Scythia and Arabia fell to Taurus, *India to Gemini.*

Now the parallel problem in ecclesiastical lore is the division
of the world amongst the twelve apostles, so that each shall
have his own sphere of labour. The writer of the Acta knows
this problem. He opens his story with it : lots are cast : *India
falls to Thomas.* The ecclesiastical division of the world has
been subordinated to the astrological. The Gnostics of Edessa
were students of the starry heavens : they knew not only their
Zodiac, but the potencies of the signs : this knowledge is
betrayed by the author of the Acta in his literary creations.
The genesis of the Thomas story is now reasonably clear, both
as regards Edessa and India.

In conclusion I will add some considerations which suggest
that the Greek Church had the same doctrine as the Syrian

Church with regard to the equivalence of Judas and Thomas. I mean that either they used the translated Acts of Thomas as an authority for the equivalence, or they had arrived at the same result by some other means. The calendar shows traces of the belief.

On June 19th the Greek Church keeps the memory of S. Jude the Apostle, who is declared to be one of the Seventy. That he is meant to be regarded as the Lord's brother and as the apostle of some city or country is evident from the language of the Synaxarium,

οὗτος παρ' αὐτοῦ τοῦ Χριστοῦ πεμφθεὶς ὡς ἀδελφὸς καὶ μυσταγωγός...

On the 20th of June is the festival of the translation of the relics of S. Thomas. Obviously there stood once side by side the festival of S. Thomas and of his relics. Thus S. Jude is S. Thomas in the Greek point of view. The festival of Judas Thomas is therefore the 19th of June. We shall see presently that another important displacement of the Dioscuri in the Western Church occurs on this very day, as well as a displacement of less importance on the previous day.

CHAPTER III.

PROTASIUS AND GERVASIUS.

LET us now pass on to examine a third case of twin saints in the Christian calendar, and test it, as in the previous instances, for Dioscurism. We will take the case of S. Protasius and S. Gervasius, the martyrs of Milan. The history of these saints is especially important in the discussion of the so-called ecclesiastical miracles, inasmuch as the marvel of the discovery of the bodies of the saints is attested by S. Ambrose, to whom their locality was revealed in a vision, and the extraordinary cures wrought by the relics are emphasized by S. Augustine as well as by many others. So that a disbelief in the miracles of Protasius and Gervasius might involve suspicion as to the veracity and reputation for good sense of the most famous doctors of the Church.

Now in approaching the subject we begin in the same way as we did with Florus and Laurus. We suspect from the assonance of the names that the saints are twins[1].

In order to verify this point, we must turn to the history of the martyrs. Here the main authorities are two, (i) a letter from Ambrose to his sister, explaining how he made the discovery of the relics, (ii) another letter, or discourse, ascribed to Ambrose, but commonly removed by the editors as being due to another hand, and printed as a supplement to the genuine works of Ambrose. In this latter composition we shall find many interesting statements belonging to the legendary development of the history of the martyrs. We shall not need,

---

[1] This suggestion is due, in the first instance, to my friend Mr T. R. Glover, to whom I am indebted for a number of valuable hints and references.

for our present purpose, to make any strong line of demarcation between the two writings: but, for convenience, we will call the second writer pseudo-Ambrose.

Now the description in ps.-Ambrose[1] records how with the bodies there was found a document from the hand of a Christian named Philip, who had stolen the bodies of the martyrs from Ravenna, where they were actually put to death, and brought them to Milan, where he buried them in his own garden if not in his own house. The document begins,

Ego servus Christi Philippus intra domum meam sanctorum corpora, quae cum filio meo rapui, sepelivi. Quorum mater Valeria et pater Vitalis sunt dicti: quos uno ortu geminos genuere, et unum Protasium, alterum Gervasium vocaverunt.

Here we have our suspicion as to the names justified.

In a similar manner we may interpret the description of the saints which we find in the Ambrosian Liturgy:

Aeterne Deus qui militibus tuis pro tui nominis amore certantibus virtutem fidei contulisti, inter quos et pios fratres BB. Protasium et Gervasium aggregare dignatus es, quos pater dudum praecesserat, adeptus martyrii palmam. Hi sunt qui vexillo coelesti signati, victricia apostoli arma sumpserunt....O quam felix germanitas! quae sacris inhaerendo eloquiis, nullo potuit interpolari contagio! O quam gloriosa certaminis causa, ubi pariter coronantur, quos unus uterus maternus effudit.

Here again the terms 'brotherhood' (germanitas) and 'born of one womb' are not to be understood in the general, but in the special sense. Cf. *uno ortu geminos genuere* in the letter of Philip quoted above.

Having settled that Protasius and Gervasius are twins, we must next examine for the characteristic features of the Dioscuri.

According to ps.-Ambrose, the vision which was seen by the Milanese saint was such that he beheld with his eyes open "duos iuvenes ephebos vestibus candidissimis, id est colobio et pallio indutos, caligulis calceatos, manibus extensis orantes." Ambrose describes the bodies which were found as follows:

Invenimus mirae magnitudinis viros duos, ut prisca aetas ferebat Ossa omnia integra, sanguinis plurimum.

[1] Migne, *P.L.* xvii., col. 744.

Now suppose we compare with these descriptions of the martyrs, dead and living, the account which Dionysius of Halicarnassus gives of the appearance of the Dioscuri at the battle of the Lake Regillus. (Dionys. VI. 13.)

ἐν ταύτῃ λέγονται τῇ μάχῃ Ποστομίῳ τε τῷ δικτάτορι καὶ τοῖς περὶ αὐτὸν τεταγμένοις ἱππεῖς δύο φανῆναι, κάλλει τε καὶ μεγέθει μακρῷ κρείττους ὧν ἡ καθ' ἡμᾶς φύσις ἐκφέρει· ἐναρχόμενοι γενειᾶν, ἡγούμενοί τε τῆς 'Ρωμαικῆς ἵππου.

And again when the Brethren appear in the Forum at the close of the day, we are told that

ἐν τῇ 'Ρωμαίων ἀγορᾷ τὸν αὐτὸν τρόπον ὀφθῆναι δύο νεανίσκοι λέγονται, πολεμικὰς ἐνδεδυκότες στολάς, μήκιστοί τε καὶ κάλλιστοι καὶ τὴν αὐτὴν ἡλικίαν ἔχοντες.

Here we have a secure series of parallels, of which the most interesting perhaps is Ambrose's

mirae magnitudinis, ut prisca aetas ferebat

with Dionysius'

μεγέθει μακρῷ κρείττους ὧν ἡ καθ' ἡμᾶς φύσις ἐκφέρει.

We may also compare for the size of the saints the description of the theophany of the Dioscuri given by Plutarch[1],

ὤφθησαν ἀπὸ στράτου μικρὸν ὕστερον ἄνδρες δύο καλοὶ καὶ μεγάλοι· τούτους εἴκασαν εἶναι Διοσκόρους,

and the similar account in Valerius Maximus[2] when, in the Macedonian war, P. Vatinius thought he saw "duos iuvenes excellentis formae albis equis residentes," who said that Paullus had captured King Perses[3].

There can be no doubt, I think, that the descriptions of both Ambrose and ps.-Ambrose are reflections of the Roman conception of the Dioscuri: and from the military touches in the accounts, as well as from the coincidences in the language, the martyrs are copied from the great twin-brethren of the battle of the Lake Regillus, and are meant to be regarded as soldiers.

---

[1] *Aemilius Paullus*, 25.
[2] *De Miraculis*, I. 8. 1.
[3] See also Aug. *De civ. Dei*, IV. 27.

And indeed Ambrose betrays the same thought elsewhere, and enables us to see that when the martyrs were recovered it was for polemical purposes, and not, as at first sight appears, in order that he might have bones of sufficient sanctity to place under the high altar of a new basilica.

He gives thanks that the martyrs have come to life to protect and defend the Church ;

Cognoscant omnes quales ego propugnatores requiram, qui propugnare possint, impugnare non soleant. Hos ego acquisivi tibi, plebs sancta, qui prosint omnibus, nemini noceant. Tales ego ambio defensores, tales milites habeo [l. aveo] : hoc est, non saeculi milites, sed milites Christi.

This is part of one of the sermons delivered by Ambrose immediately after he had brought the relics of the martyrs to light; and it shows pretty clearly that Ambrose himself had the Dioscuri in mind, when he recovered the martyrs and put them in the forefront in the battle with the Arians. That this is the meaning of the military figures and language may be gathered from what Ambrose says about the strife which was immediately provoked between the Arians and the Catholics over the supposed relics and the miracles which were wrought over them. The martyrs would have nothing to do with the Arians, and the Arians would have nothing to do with the martyrs. To their credit it should be said that the Arians denounced both the discovery of the relics and the miracles as frauds; and to the credit of S. Ambrose it should be said that he tells us plainly that the Arians were not taken in by his visions nor by his gigantic bones nor by his sarcophagus with its miracle-working blood in which the people were, by thousands, dipping their pocket-handkerchiefs.

I do not mean that Ambrose in thus emphasizing the military character of his protégés did not want to find martyrs; on the contrary it had been matter of lamentation to him that the Church at Milan was short of the means of grace. And in the fervour of the discovery he writes to his sister, in order to inform her on the point:

Iam in numerum martyrum diu ante ignorati Protasius Gervasiusque praeferuntur, qui sterilem martyribus ecclesiam Mediolanensem iam pluri-

morum matrem filiorum laetari passionis propriae fecerint et titulis et
exemplis.

But the martyrs did much more than cause the Church
at Milan to multiply: they made the increase at the cost of
the Arians, and the discovery has, therefore, the highest theological value. The Arians were like the Latin forces at the
battle of the Lake Regillus: they suddenly found opposed to
them two men in white who were leading the Roman line of
advance. And Ambrose who put them in the front of the
battle knew that he was parading the Dioscuri in a Christian
dress.

The first sermon that he made to the excited populace over
the newly found relics was on the 19th Psalm (Caeli enarrant).
He explains how 'night unto night showeth forth knowledge.'
First of all he allegorizes that 'night unto night' means 'flesh
unto flesh,' the flesh being apparently the recovered bodies.
Then he breaks out:

> Bonae noctes, noctes lucidae, *quae habent stellas.* Sicut enim stella
> a stella differt in claritate, ita et resurrectio mortuorum.

He then proceeds to explain that the resurrection is the
recovery of the martyrs, who have come to light to defend the
Church. In my judgment, both the selection of the Psalm and
the allusion to the martyrs as stars is a further suggestion that
he had the Dioscuri in mind[1].

But there is another curious confirmation of the correctness
of our interpretation in the calendar itself. We have pointed
out that Protase and Gervase in the East are celebrated on the
14th of October. Now suppose we look at the previous day
in the calendar, and see who is commemorated. We shall find
amongst the saints for the day a certain *Dioscoros*: and upon
examination of his record, we shall find little more than that
he confessed the Christian faith before a governor named
Lukianos: we have already met this gentleman in the legends

---

[1] I see that some writers are disposed to treat the recovery of the bodies as a
happy accident: "a chance excavation might easily be rewarded by a discovery
of two bodies" (v. *Dict. Christ. Biog.* s. v. Gervasius and Ambrosius). Not
if *two* bodies were being looked for, and big ones.

of Thomas. So we shall conclude that Dioscoros stands for the Dioscuri, and the probability is that he has been pushed back a day to make room for Protase and Gervase. His appearance in their neighbourhood is significant. Upon the whole, then, the genesis of the festival of Protasius and Gervasius is clearly made out. They are good Christians, no doubt, but they were once saints in a different order of beliefs and worships. They have transferred their allegiance from Olympus to Mount Zion.

We have now demonstrated that (i) Protasius and Gervasius were twins, and (ii) that they stand for the Dioscuri.

And now let us turn again to the calendar.

The Western calendar commemorates Protasius and Gervasius on June 19th. The Eastern Church (see the Basilian Menology) transfers the saints, with two other Milanese worthies, to Oct. 14th. But then there is another curious transference in the opposite direction; for we shall find that the Eastern Church commemorates on June 19th the fame of S. Jude, the Lord's brother, while the Latins have transferred S. Jude to Oct. 28, and have coupled him with S. Simon.

Now, remembering what we found out with regard to the displacement of the Dioscuri in Edessa, by Judas Thomas, we can hardly fail to be struck by the coincidences which the calendar shows, in making June 19th a day of the Dioscuri in both the East and West; and in showing very nearly the same phenomenon occurring in October. This can hardly be accidental, and it may be taken as a striking confirmation of our theory that Protasius and Gervasius stand for the Dioscuri, when we find another well-known displacement of the Dioscuri on the same day in the Greek Church.

Suppose now we turn to the previous day in the calendar, June 18th. It is the day of celebration of S. Sebastian, of the saints Marcus and Marcellianus, and others. We naturally enquire whether the pair of similar names covers another case of twins, and if so, whether there are any Dioscuric features about them. A reference to the Acta Sanctorum at once settles the first point:

Clarissimi viri Marcus et Marcellianus, *gemini fratres*, cum servis suis tenti et in vinculis constituti.

Their father attempts to turn them away from the Christian faith : he cries out,

O filii! baculus senectutis meae et *geminum lumen*, cur sic mortem diligitis ?

But the blessed Sebastian protests and encourages the brothers to martyrdom :

Non separabuntur a vobis, sed *vadunt in caelum parare vobis sidereas mansiones.*

After language like this, we can scarcely avoid the conclusion that there is another Roman festival of the Dioscuri on June 18th.

We drew attention above to the language of Ambrose in his first sermon on the recovery of the martyrs, when he took for his text the 19th Psalm, and proceeded to explain who were the stars of the heaven that declares the glory of God. It is perhaps conventional to treat the martyrs as constellations, and conventional too to preach about them from the Psalm in question. It may, however, be worth while comparing the language and method of S. Ambrose with the language of S. Chrysostom in preaching on S. Thomas and the language of the Greek Menaeum in speaking of S. Jude.

When Chrysostom made the celebration of S. Thomas' festival the occasion for a discourse against the Arians, he treated his saint in the following manner :

εἰς πᾶσαν τὴν γῆν ἐξῆλθεν ἡ δόξα αὐτοῦ, καὶ εἰς τὰ πέρατα τῆς οἰκουμένης τὰ τρόπαια αὐτοῦ. πῶς οὖν αὐτὸν ὀνομάσω; ἥλιον; ἀλλ' ὑπὸ νυκτὸς οὐκ ἐλέγχεται. ἀστέρα; ἀλλ' ἡμέρα τοῦτον οὐ κρύπτει. ἐν παντὶ καιρῷ καταυγάζει τὴν κτίσιν· πάντα ζόφον ἀπελαύνει τῆς οἰκουμένης.

The Menaea say much the same of S. Jude: he is the spiritual heaven that discourses the glory of God (ὁ θεόπτης φθέγγεται, οὐρανός τις ὥσπερ λογικός, τοῦ θεοῦ τὴν δόξαν, διηγούμενος τοῦ δι' ἡμᾶς ἐν σαρκὶ φανέντος θαύματα).

He becomes a second sun, conformed to the radiance of the first Sun (Λόγον τὸν σαρκωθέντα εὑρὼν διδάσκαλον καὶ ταῖς τούτου, θεόπτα, μαρμαρυγαῖς πυρούμενος, ἐγένου φῶς δεύτερον, ταῖς τοῦ πρώτου λάμψεσι συμμορφούμενος).

And he is said to drive away the darkness from the creation (κατεφώτισας εὐσεβῶν καρδίας, καὶ τὸν ἐπικείμενον τῇ κτίσει σκοτασμὸν ἀπεδιώξας).

The language and ideas are strikingly coincident, and very well suited to saints who are displacements of well-known Greek stars. Especially striking is the description of S. Jude as a δεύτερος ἥλιος : we must not, however, build on this. It is probably conventional. Other saints, as S. Euthymius, are addressed in the same way. And the fragments of hymns in the Menaea have a tendency to repetition.

But the case of Chrysostom is different, and it almost looks as if he had some knowledge of the previous ecclesiastical history of the saint whom he was celebrating. However, as we have said, matters of this kind readily become conventional, and it is quite possible that Chrysostom and Ambrose may have done the regular and expected thing when they quoted the 19th Psalm and used it to illustrate the glory of the saints and martyrs of the Church.

It may be thought appropriate, at the close of the investigation into the meaning of the cult of Protase and Gervase, to remind ourselves again that we have been discussing a historical problem which is closely involved with certain theological problems which are still held to be of supreme importance.

The story of the finding of the relics of these martyrs and of the miracles which profusely followed the discovery, is connected with the ecclesiastical reaction against Arianism which brought the church at Milan, under the leadership of Ambrose, out of the power of the Empress Justina and her followers. We need not therefore be surprised at the attempts which have been made to guarantee these heaven-disclosed relics and the miracles to which they gave occasion. It was natural enough that the late Cardinal Newman should select such an incident as a controversial position of the first importance. And it will be, at least, edifying to read over again, in the light of our observations on the meaning of the festivals and dates of the calendar, the elaborate and ingenious essays in which he protected the reputation of Ambrose, Augustine and Paulinus, and the ecclesiastical miracles for which they stand sponsors.

Reference should be made to the articles on 'Primitive Christianity' which Newman contributed to the *British Magazine* between the years 1833 and 1836, in which will be found a sketch of the situation at Milan and an intimation of the way in which that situation was changed by Ambrose's discovery.

With this should be compared the famous 'Essays on Ecclesiastical Miracles,' in which a whole section is devoted to the Recovery of the Blind Man by the Relics of S. Gervasius and S. Protasius at Milan.

To do Newman justice, we transcribe from the essays on 'Primitive Christianity' his summing up of the whole question.

I want to know what reason there is for stumbling at the above narrative, which will not throw uncertainty upon the very fact that there was such a Bishop as Ambrose, or such an Empress as Justina, or such a heresy as the Arian, or any Church at all in Milan. Let us consider some of the circumstances under which it comes to us.

1. We have the concordant evidence of three distinct witnesses, of whom at least two were on the spot when the alleged miracles were wrought, one writing at the time, another some years afterwards in a distant country. And the third [Paulinus], writing after an interval of twenty-six years, agrees minutely with the evidence of the two former, not adding to the miraculous narrative, as is the manner of those who lose their delicate care for exactness in their admiration of the things and persons of whom they speak.

2. The miracle is wrought in public, on a person well-known, on one who continued to live in the place where it was professedly wrought, and who, by devoting himself to the service of the martyrs who were the instruments of his cure, was a continual memorial of the mercy which he professed to have received, and challenged enquiry into it, and refutation if that were possible.

3. Ambrose, one of our informants, publicly appealed, at the time when the occurrence took place, to the general belief, claimed it for the miracle, and that in a sermon which is still extant.

4. He made his statement in the presence of most bitter and most powerful enemies, who were much concerned, and very able to expose the fraud, if there was one ; who did, as might be expected, deny the hand of God in the matter ; but who, for all that appears, did nothing but deny what they could not consistently confess, without ceasing to be what they were.

5. A great and practical impression was made upon the popular mind in consequence of the alleged miracles : or, in the words of a

historian [Gibbon] whose very vocation it is to disbelieve them, 'Their effect on the minds of the people was rapid and irresistible : and the feeble sovereign of Italy found himself unable to contend with the favourite of heaven.'

6. And so powerfully did all this press upon the Court, that, as the last words of this extract intimate, the persecution was given up, and the Catholics left in quiet possession of the Churches.

On the whole, then, are we not in the following dilemma ? If the miracle did not take place, then S. Ambrose and S. Augustine, men of name, said they had ascertained a fact which they did not ascertain, and said it in the face of enemies, with an appeal to a whole city, and that continued during a quarter of a century. What instrument of refutation shall we devise against a case like this, neither so violently *à priori* as to supersede the testimony of Evangelists, nor so fastidious of evidence as to imperil Tacitus or Caesar ? On the other hand, if the miracle did take place, a certain measure of authority, more or less, must surely attach to S. Ambrose,—to his doctrine and his life, to his ecclesiastical principles, to the Church itself of the fourth century, of which he is one main pillar. The miracle gives a certain sanction to three things at once, to the Catholic doctrine of the Trinity, to the Church's resistance of the civil power and to the Commemoration of Saints and Martyrs.

Thus far the great Oxford leader. His foundations appear to be hardly commensurate with the superstructure. But it is a good case for a study of the laws of evidence and of the nature of belief: and we have heard it said that "it is not contrary to experience that testimony should be false."

"Amicus Ambrosius, magis amica Veritas."

CHAPTER IV.

SPEUSIPPUS, ELASIPPUS AND MESIPPUS.

THE Greek calendar contains, under the date Jan. 16th, the memorial of three saints and their grandmother. Their names, as given in the printed Menaeum, are

Peusippus, Elasippus, and Mesippus:

and their grandmother is called Neonilla.

So they stand also in the printed Synaxaristes; but we must evidently correct Peusippus to Σπεύσιππος, and as this agrees closely with Ἐλάσιππος in meaning, we shall probably be correct in treating Μέσιππος as corrupt, and restoring some related form. But whether this change be required or not, the student of the calendar will be struck by the similarity of the structure of the names. What does it mean? Are they three converted jockeys, or may we apply the method which we used in the interpretation of Florus and Laurus and say that they are triplets? At first sight this latter hypothesis seems very improbable.

The heading of their festival in the Menaeum is as follows:

Μνήμη τῶν ἁγίων μαρτύρων καὶ αὐταδέλφων, Πευσίππου, Ἐλασίππου καὶ Μεσίππου· καὶ Νεονίλλης τῆς μάμμης αὐτῶν.

Here it is conceded that the three saints are brothers, and the suspicion arises of a closer relationship; for it has been already pointed out that αὐτάδελφος in this branch of literature means often the same thing as δίδυμος.

When we examine more closely into the account given in the Menaeum, we find the following memorial verses:

Κἂν ὦσιν ἱππεῖς, κλήσεων σημασίᾳ
Πέζοι τρέχουσι τρίδυμοι τρεῖς πρὸς φλόγα.

Here we expressly have them described as a triplet of brothers who are horsemen. The verses are the echo of the account given in the embedded Synaxarion:

Οὗτοι ὑπῆρχον ἐκ Καππαδοκίας τρίδυμοι, πωλοδαμνεῖν ἄριστα μεμαθηκότες, καὶ τοὺς ἵππους κατὰ τῶν πεδίων κινεῖν.

The Synaxaristes turns the same statement into modern Greek in the following style:

Οὗτοι οἱ ἅγιοι κατήγοντο ἐκ τῆς Καππαδοκίας, γεννηθέντες καὶ οἱ τρεῖς συγχρόνως, ἐκ τῆς αὐτῆς κοιλίας· ἦσαν δὲ ἐπιτηδειότατοι εἰς τὸ νὰ ἡμερόνωσι καὶ νὰ ἱππεύωσι τοὺς νέους καὶ ἀγρίους ἵππους, καὶ νὰ τρέχωσιν ἐπ᾽ αὐτῶν εἰς τὴν πεδιάδα.

So there can be no doubt that the triplicity of the names implies triplets. But we have also from the names and from the legends the connexion of the triplet with horses. If there had been only two of them, we should have unhesitatingly made the identification with the Dioscuri. But what are we to say, when they appear as three instead of two and when the lady who accompanies them is their grandmother?

In the first place, observe that the perplexity in which we find ourselves is one in which archeologists were already involved. For example at Brasiae in Laconia there were three statues with caps in the manner of the Dioscuri, accompanied by Athena; Pausanias was unable to decide whether they were meant for the Dioscuri or the Corybantes. And the same thing occurs on certain Etruscan mirrors (Röscher s.v. *Dioscuri* 1177)[1] where there are three figures of men with the pilos and one woman. Cicero, too, knew the Dioscuri as a triad[2]:

Διόσκουροι etiam apud Graios multis modis nominantur, primi tres qui appellantur Anactes Athenis, ex rege Iove antiquissimo et Proserpina nati, Tritopatreus, Eubuleus, Dionysus; secundi Iovi tertio nati et Leda, Castor et Pollux : tertii dicuntur a nonnullis Alco, Melampus et Tmolus, Atrei filii qui Pelope natus fuit.

Here we have a clear recognition of the fact that the Dioscuri were sometimes regarded as a triad. The same thing is true of the Kabiri with whom they are closely connected.

---

[1] See also Albert, *Castor et Pollux en Italie*, p. 135.
[2] *De Nat. Deorum*, III. 21, § 53.

So there is every probability that we have to do with a local variation of the cult, say in Cappadocia. Then we come to the question of the grandmother. On reading the story of the martyrdom more closely, we come to the following additional points. The martyrs had invited their grandmother to a heathen festival of their own country, in honour of Zeus Nemesios. The grandmother was already a Christian and reviled the idols that her family worshipped. Persuaded by her, they likewise became Christians and were promptly committed to the flames by the local rulers.

The only clue that this furnishes to the unravelling of the legend is the statement as to the displaced cult, and this is commonly a trustworthy piece of information. If, then, the displaced festival was one of Zeus Nemesios, then the female figure should be that of Nemesis, who has been locally regarded as the grandmother of the Dioscuri. That Nemesis comes into the cycle of the legends of the Dioscuri we already knew. Pausanias, in his description of the famous statue of Nemesis at Rhamnus, tells us that Nemesis was reckoned to be *the mother* of Helen, and Leda was only her nurse. On the base of the statue are carved, amongst other figures, the Dioscuri. So there is no real difficulty in the supposition that Nemesis might be regarded locally as the *grandmother* of the Dioscuri and the *mother* of Leda. We notice, further, that on the face of the monument where the Dioscuri are described, there is a third figure holding a horse. Pausanias describes the sculptures as follows: πεποίηκε δὲ Τυνδάρεών τε καὶ τοὺς παῖδας καὶ ἄνδρα σὺν ἵππῳ παρεστηκότα, Ἱππέα ὄνομα. The third figure is, then, named Hippeus, which is quite in the manner of the Cappadocian nomenclature of the three saints.

Reviewing the argument, we may suggest that, somewhere in Cappadocia, a cult of Nemesis and the Dioscuri was displaced by a Christian ritual. Nemesis was probably regarded locally as the *grandmother* of the Dioscuri, and the latter were thought of as a triplet and not as a pair.

If this explanation be correct, we have a fifth case of the survival of the Dioscuri in Christian tradition.

CHAPTER V.

S. KASTOULOS AND S. POLYEUCTES.

Suppose now that we follow the clue suggested to us in the foregoing pages, the observed fact, that is, of the occurrence of the Heavenly Twins in the calendar and the detection of their sister in the immediate neighbourhood. We may go on to ask whether there are any cases in which the Twins themselves have been separated and are yet adjacent to one another in the calendar, or where one exists without the other.

The Greek calendar, for example, will show us a celebration on Dec. 18th of a certain Kastoulos. Upon examination of his record, we find that, after appropriate tortures, he was thrown into a pit. Remembering that this was also the end of Florus and Laurus, we are suspicious that Kastoulos is a disguise of Kastor. And when we scrutinize the calendar in the neighbourhood, we find that on the very next day there is a celebration of Polyeuctes, and we naturally conclude that the names are conjugate, and that they stand for Kastor and Polydeuces. And it will be necessary to scan the calendar carefully for all the occurrences of names resembling Kastor and Polydeuces, in order that we may recognize any local cults that are the successors of the ancient worship of the great twin-brethren. Meanwhile, in thus stumbling upon Polyeuctes, we have before us a most interesting problem; for not only does this name turn up several times in the ecclesiastical year, but there is one famous martyr of the name, over whose legend there has been a long controversy, as to whether it was all legend and no history, or whether there was a historical basis underlying the different forms in which the legend has come down to us.

We start upon the enquiry with a very strong bias against the belief in any historical foundation at all. The disguise of the adjacent names is so thin, that all the conditions of the question are satisfied by saying that Dec. 18th is one of the days on which, in some locality or localities not yet identified, there was especial devotion to the twin-brethren. The locality may, indeed, be hard to fix; for Kastoulos (whom the Synaxaristes naïvely calls Kastor in one place) is thrown into the entourage of S. Sebastian, and Polyeuctes is said to belong to Caesarea in Cappadocia. Probably the best way to determine whether Polyeuctes (either in Cappadocia or elsewhere) is a real person will be by examining the greatest of the saints who bear the name, and testing his legend in the light of the suspicion which we have expressed above.

Polyeuctes the Great, if we may define him so, is the patron saint of Melitene in Armenia (the modern Malatia). His cult must be very early, for we find a section devoted to him in Gregory of Tours, who also tells us of the prominence of the saint in the Church of Constantinople, as well as of the diffusion of the cult in the churches in France. Let us see what Gregory says on the point. He begins by telling us why Polyeuctes was honoured in Constantinople: *it was as the avenger of perjury.*

> Apud Constantinopolin vero magno cultu Polioctus martyr colitur, pro co praecipue quod cum magnis virtutibus polleat, *in periuris* tamen *praesens ultor existit.*   (*De glor. Mart.* 103.)

And the same information is given for the French churches when describing an agreement made between certain French princes:

> Ecce pactiones quae inter nos factae sunt, ut quisquis sine fratris voluntate Parisios[1] urbem ingrederetur, amitteret partem suam, essetque

---

[1] In 1711, in excavating in the choir of Notre Dame, an altar was discovered, on two faces of which were representations of Castor and Pollux. Here we have the archeological proof of their cult in Paris, along with two other Celtic (?) deities. (See Albert, l.c. p. 52.)

Polioctus martyr, cum Hilario atque Martino confessoribus, iudex ac
retributor eius.   (*Hist. Franc.* VII. 6.)

Now how could a martyr of Melitene become in such a
short space of time the avenger of perjury in both East and
West? It could only be possible if he had displaced an avenger
of perjury already existing both in East and West; and the
avenger of perjury is naturally the person by whom one swears.
'So help me God' means 'as God shall save me,' and implies
that God deals out damnation when deserved. When, therefore, we find that an appeal lies to Polyeuctes, we at once say,
in view of the suspicion with which we started,

Edepol and *Mecastor.*

And a little reflection will show that the natural way to
stop the popular swearing by Castor and Pollux was to transfer
the oaths to saints who should sound the same. Viewed in
this light the statements of S. Gregory of Tours are perfectly
intelligible, and we are confirmed in our belief that Polyeuctes
is Polydeuces[1].

But this does not absolutely exclude the belief that there
may be a person behind the legend, for Polyeuctes is a possible
name, apart from substitution and invention.

[1] Adjuration to the Twins in Greek was commonly under the form νὴ τὼ θεώ.
Thus in Xenophon, *Hellenica* IV. 4. 10, Pasimachus the Spartan swears in
Doric, Ναὶ τὼ σιώ, 'Αργεῖοι. And in *Anab.* VI. 6. 34, Cleandros the Spartan
swears in the same form. Here the two gods are Castor and Polydeuces.

But in Aristophanes, *Acharnians* 905, the Boeotian uses the form νεὶ τὼ σιώ,
where the gods are Amphion and Zethus.

That the Celts used also to observe the cult of the twin-brethren (which is
suggested by the invocation of Polioctus at Paris) appears from Diodorus Siculus
(IV. 56) δεικνύντες τοὺς παρὰ τὸν 'Ωκεανὸν κατοικοῦντας σεβομένους μάλιστα τῶν θεῶν
τοὺς Διοσκόρους.

In Rome swearing by Castor was originally a woman's oath, but the oath by
the Twins gradually became taken up by men, at first in the form of Aedepol
(see Aulus Gellius, XI. 6: "Paulatim tamen, inscitia antiquitatis, viros dicere
aedepol coepisse").

See Albert's interesting chapter on Castor and Pollux as the gods of com-
merce and good faith; "pouvait-on mieux protester de sa bonne foi qu'en
invoquant les dieux qui la personnifaient ou le temple qui semblait en être le
sanctuaire favori?" This assumes that Aedepol = per aedem Pollucis.

When we turn to the legend, we find that it is certainly a very beautiful one, and takes high rank in the literature of hagiology, so as to have worthily attracted the dramatic skill of Corneille.

The story opens with the recitation of the affectionate relations that subsisted between Polyeuctes and his friend Nearchus. The narrator at the very outset apologises for the fact that they are not brothers. He describes them as ἀδελφοὶ μέν, οὐ κατὰ γένος, ἀλλὰ κατὰ προαίρεσιν. This gratuitous explanation betrays what he is doing: he is working over a story of two brothers whom he has turned into two friends. He explains how dear they were to one another. One was a Christian, Nearchus; the other, Polyeuctes, nominally a pagan. An imperial edict against the Christians has been published, and Nearchus is broken-hearted, because he has a prospect of martyrdom which his friend cannot share. The dialogue which ensues between the friends is a beautiful one. As the Latin Acts sum the matter up,

Hoc optat fratri quod sibi quoque, si aliter se res habuisset, optaret. *Non vult solus ire ad gloriam,* ne plenitudini beatitudinis suae aliquid derogandum crederet, si hac solus et sine socio frui videretur.

(Aubé, *Polyeucte,* p. 106.)

So one brother would not go to heaven without the other; but this is what the Greek moralists knew how to dwell upon in the story of Kastor and Polydeuces. It was one of the favourite texts in preaching disinterested love. The appeal of the immortal Twin on behalf of the mortal one has been imitated, and the result is Nearchus' lamentation over Polyeuctes. The best illustration will perhaps be Plutarch, *De Fraterno Amore (Moral.* 589),

ὁ δὲ Πολυδεύκης οὐδὲ θεὸς ἠθέλησε μόνος, ἀλλὰ μᾶλλον ἡμίθεος σὺν τῷ ἀδελφῷ γενέσθαι, καὶ τῆς θνητῆς μερίδος μετασχεῖν ἐπὶ τῷ μεταδοῦναι τῆς ἀθανασίας ἐκείνῳ.

When Nearchus has explained the situation to his friend, he is comforted to find that Polyeuctes has already had a vision which has resulted in his conversion. Christ has appeared to him, and finding him (as the Dioscuri naturally

would be found) in military dress, has taken from him his
torn and worn chlamys, and replaced it by a new chlamys of
silk with a gold buckle, and has given him a winged horse on
which he is to ride to heaven[1].

We see at once the origin of the military dress and the
winged horse, which latter quadruped has been a serious
difficulty to the transcribers, whose explanations have crept
into the text here and there.

Thus the moment we apply our touchstone to the story,
the historical elements fade away into legend. The remaining
details concern only the trial, when Polyeuctes has to face the
appeals and reproaches of his father-in-law Felix and his wife
Paulina; he is, of course, mercilessly tortured and finally
decapitated. But there is no need to examine the matter
more closely. All the history that there is in the account is
limited to the fact that the Dioscuri were worshipped in
Melitene, and that their worship was early replaced by a
Christian cult.

Aubé has made a vigorous attempt to prove that the
personages in the legend are real; he published some unedited
forms of the Greek and Latin Martyrdoms of Polyeuctes, with
the view of showing that the Acta were in the main trustworthy. His historical minimum of real persons includes
Nearchus, Polyeuctes, Felix and Paulina. Their social position
and relationships are also to be depended on. The edict of
Valerian against the Christians is historical; so is the back-
wardness of the Christians, and the forwardness of Polyeuctes,
who destroys the pagan idols, the efforts of Felix to save his
son-in-law, the intervention of Paulina and the decapitation of
the saint.

But we have the matter in a different light now. And
there is no reason for yielding to the temptation to believe
that a story must be true for which we find some fresh
documentary evidence!

---

[1] "Sordidam sedem (?) quandam ab eo sustulerat cum chlamyde militari":
and cf. the Greek Acts, as published by Aubé:

οὗτος προσελθὼν ἐμοὶ τὴν μὲν ῥυπαρὰν ταύτην καὶ ἀνθρωπίνην χλαμύδα περι-
εῖλεν ἀπ' ἐμοῦ κτέ.

It only remains to scrutinize the dates which are furnished by the Greek Acts.

The text says that the martyrdom is the 9th of January ;

$$\text{ἐν ἡμέρᾳ τετράδι ἐννάτῃ τοῦ Ἰανουαρίου.}$$

There seems to be something wrong about this, and one would at first suspect that τετράδι should be corrected to δεκάτῃ, so as to make the martyrdom Jan. 19th.

The Greek appendix to the Acts, however, says that they are to be read twice in the year: viz. the IV. Id. Jan. (= Jan. 10), the day of the death; and VIII. Kal. Jan. (= Dec. 25), the day when cloths, soaked in the martyr's blood, were brought to the city of the Cananeotae. This does not help us much, as we do not know what city it is: the former date is nearly the same as in the text.

The Bollandists give the date as Feb. 13th, for the Western Church. But they also know of a celebration which seems to belong to the same cycle

on May 19th⎫
and May 21st⎭ at Caesarea in Cappadocia

and at some unknown places on Jan. 8th and Jan. 11th.

On the whole we have not yet succeeded in clearing up the meaning of the dates. They are, no doubt, those of certain local Dioscoric festivals.

From the existence of festivals on Jan. 8 and Jan. 10, the probability is that after all Jan. 9 is the right date for the festival at Melitene.

But there is also confirmation of the correctness of the date Feb. 13. For on this day in the West they celebrated the memory of a presbyter at Trèves whose name was Castor. So here also the conjugate saint is found in the calendar.

It will be convenient if we exhibit in a tabular form some of the functions of the principal groups of saints whom we have been discussing, as compared with those of the Açvins and the Dioscuri.

Functions of Twins.

	Açvins	Dioscuri	Amphion and Zethus	Florus and Laurus	Judas Thomas	Protase and Gervase	Speusippus, Elasippus, and Mesippus	Nearchus and Polyeuctes ?
Darkness-dispellers	+	+						
Helpers in battle	+	+				+		+
Healers (blind, lame, &c.)	+	+		+	+	+		
Sexual helpers	+	+			+			
Saviours from sea	+	+			+			
Horse-riders, horse-tamers, and ass-tamers	+	+	+	+	+		+	+
Makers of ploughs and yokes	+	+			+			
Builders		+	+	+	+			
Immortal and mortal			+	+	+			+

The results arrived at in the previous pages are surprising in the disclosures which they make of the extent and variety of the worship of the twin-brethren. It was popular worship, universal worship.

As in other and similar cases, the literature of the world is an inadequate guide to the knowledge of its religion. And in the case of the Dioscuri, this seems to have been especially so. The cult retained much of its primitive simplicity: temples appear to have been few, monuments very simple; but, in spite of this simplicity, and perhaps because of it, the popular religion was deeply tinctured with Dioscurism.

Dion Chrysostom betrays this fact when he says that in his day everyone still believed the Dioscuri were deities:

Orat. LXI. 11 (Chryseis).

Κάστωρ καὶ Πολυδεύκης οἱ Διὸς παῖδες ἐνομίσθησαν καὶ θεοὶ μέχρι νῦν πᾶσι δοκοῦσι διὰ τὴν δύναμιν ἣν τότε ἔσχον.

The language helps us to understand the pressure on primitive Christianity in competing with popular beliefs.

We expected, when we began our investigation, to find a single festival in the calendar that could be assigned to the Twins, and the festivals have multiplied so rapidly as to surprise us.

One reason for this appears to lie in the existence of a monthly cult, going back, perhaps, to the earliest forms of human chronology.

On looking over those festivals which we have already identified we can hardly fail to be struck with the prominence given to the 18th or 19th days of the month.

For example, on

April 19th we have a festival of Dioscoros.
May 19th is a festival of Polyeuctes.
June 18th is the festival of Marcus and Marcellianus.
June 19th is the festival of Judas Thomas and of Protase and Gervase.
Aug. 18th is the festival of Florus and Laurus, and of Helena.
Sept. 18th is a festival of Kastor.
Dec. 18th is a festival of Kastoulos.
Dec. 19th is a festival of Polyeuctes—

so that for six months in the year there is a suspicion of a festival of the Brethren at the 18th or 19th of the month.

The impression which this makes upon one is that a number of the festivals belong to a connected monthly system. Thus an explanation is found, in part, of the recurrence of the cult in the calendar.

We shall probably find, as we continue the investigation on the lines suggested in the foregoing pages, that there are more cases of the displaced Twins in the calendar than those to which we have drawn attention. But life is short, and hagiology is long, and so, for the present, we desist from the enquiry.

SUPPLEMENTARY NOTE ON FLORUS AND LAURUS.

THE evidence for the connexion of Florus and Laurus with horses finds an interesting reinforcement in the following passage from Tylor's *Early History of Mankind*, to which my attention has been drawn by the author. It is important, also, as connecting the cult of the Twins with the 'needfire.'

The Western clergy discountenanced, and, as far as they could, put down the needfire; but in Russia it was not only allowed, but was (and very likely may be still) practised under ecclesiastical sanction, the priest being the chief actor in the ceremony. This interesting fact seems not to have been known to Grimm and Kühn, and the following passage, which proves it, is still further remarkable as asserting that the ancient fire-making by friction was still used in Russia for practical as well as ceremonial purposes in the last century. It is contained in an account of the adventures of four Russian sailors who were driven by a storm upon the desert island of East Spitzbergen[1].

"They knew, however, that if one rubs violently together two pieces of dry wood, one hard and the other soft, the latter will catch fire. Besides this being the way in which the Russian peasants obtain fire when they are in the woods, there is also a religious ceremony, performed in every village where there is a church, which could not have been unknown to them. Perhaps it will be not disagreeable for me here to give an account of this ceremony, though it does not belong to the story. The 18th of August, old style, is called by the Russians *Frol i Lavior*, these being the names of two martyrs, called Florus and Laurus in the Roman Kalendar: they fall, according to this latter, on the 29th of the said month, when the festival of the Beheading of John is celebrated. On this day the Russian peasants bring their horses to the village church, at the side of which they have dug the evening before a pit with two outlets. Each horse has his bridle, which is made of lime-tree bark. They let the horses, one after another, go into

[1] P. L. le Roy, *Erzählung der Begebenheiten*, Riga, 1760. (An Eng. Tr. in Pinkerton, Vol. I.)

this pit, at the opposite outlet of which the priest stands with an asperging-brush in his hand, with which he sprinkles them with holy water. As soon as the horses are come out, their bridles are taken off, and they are made to go between two fires, which are kindled with what the Russians call *Givoy agon*, that is, 'living fire,' of which I will give the explanation, after remarking that the peasants throw the bridles of the horses into one of these fires to burn them up. Here is the manner of kindling this *Givoy Agon* or living fire."

(TYLOR, Early History of Mankind, p. 257.)

We must examine whether this conjunction of Florus and Laurus with the new fire may not imply a New Year's festival with the sun in the sign Gemini.

SUPPLEMENTARY NOTE ON THE DIOSCURI IN EDESSA.

I HAVE omitted to notice on p. 33, that Julian says that the Sun was honoured in Edessa along with two subordinate deities, named Monimos and Azizos (see Duval, l. c.), and M. Cumont has maintained that the worship is Mithraic, and that Monimos and Azizos are respectively the evening star and the morning star. "Aziz désigne le Lucifer des Romains, le Phosphoros des Grecs, le dieu de l'étoile du matin, qui précède le soleil et annonce le retour de la lumière et de la vie, et qu'on représentait sous la forme d'un adolescent portant une torche" (*Revue Archéologique*, 1888, p. 96). Without introducing Mithraism, we have arrived at a similar conclusion as to the worship of Hesper-Phosphor in Edessa.

Printed in the United States
By Bookmasters